I0459323

The Lost Trails Guidebook

Vol. 4

Eastern Idaho

A Publication by BlueRibbon Coalition

Disclaimer: all information is up to date at time of printing. As a user, you are responsible to acquire the most current maps and information available.

ISBN 979-8-9870362-5-9

BLUERIBBON
COALITION

Lead Sponsor

Mapping Partner

TRAILSOFFROAD™

Contents

A shot from Blackrock Canyon near Pocatello, ID.

Introduction

During the last few years, I have flown into the airport in Boise, Idaho a handful of times. The Boise airport is relatively small, but at any given time it has at least three major advertisements for home builders in the area. I'm not talking about a small poster on a wall. These are advertisements that take up entire walls. You can't miss them. If you fly into Idaho, the message is clear: Idaho wants out-of-staters to move to Idaho.

Once you get out of the airport and out on the ground in Idaho, it doesn't take very long to learn that most Idahoans don't, in fact, want you to move there. Most locals become visibly upset when I tell them that the ads in the airport had me convinced I should come buy an affordable home in Idaho. This is now becoming an attitude that is pervasive throughout the West as western towns are inundated with floods of newcomers who have discovered one best-kept secret after another.

When we first approached the Snake River Offroaders about the idea of creating a Lost Trails Guidebook for Eastern Idaho, we were expecting to get an enthusiastic welcome to the idea. After all, the first two volumes of the guidebooks had been popular in Utah, where most of their trails and dispersed campsites were located. While some members of the club liked the idea, there were some who were not thrilled.

As we got to work on the guidebook with the locals who offered to help inventory and document many of the trails in the book, we learned that the reason the other club members were soft on the idea was because they didn't want to publicize their trails for others to come use them.

This isn't the first time we've come across this issue as we've developed and published three volumes of the Lost Trails Guidebook. There is a strong tendency to want to gatekeep our favorite places hidden within the vast acreage of our public lands. This is partially why our Lost Trails Guidebooks only provide a sampling of trails and campsites. For every trail we include, there are hundreds of miles of other trails nearby that are left out. For every campsite we include, there are dozens we don't share.

Because we think part of the value of public lands is to allow for members of the public to explore the unknown and face uncertainty and risk, we've intentionally tried to make these books more like a sample day at Costco instead of an overflowing grocery cart haul.

However, while we understand the tendency to want to limit knowledge of amazing trails, we unfortunately face a situation where trails that receive little use are the most vulnerable trails to be permanently shut down. In our Lost Trails Guidebook Volume 2, we shared 26 trails in the Moab area that we were worried might be closed. Sure enough, in 2023 when the Bureau of Land Management released their final plan for the Labyrinth Rims/Gemini Bridges area, they did end up closing 11 of these trails, along with hundreds of others.

These closures resulted in one of our biggest court fights, that at the time of writing is still unresolved. The current Trump Administration has announced a plan to reevaluate a lengthy list of closed trails. This list includes almost all of the trails that were included in Lost Trails Guidebook Volume 2. Throughout this fight, we've used their inclusion in the guidebook as a way to legitimize the recreation value of these trails and validate the need to reopen them.

While we appreciate the allure of gatekeeping trails and campsites, we can't ignore the incentives created by the legal system to publicize trails to justify keeping them open. People can't effectively fight for something they know nothing about.

Next to Utah, Idaho and Arizona are the two states that are most aggressively updating their travel management plans. We are confident that showcasing the recreation value of the trails in these states is one way we can increase public awareness and support for these trails.

And, once you ride any of these trails, we think you will want to join us and our friends in Idaho in fiercely defending the continued public access to these areas. We also believe as you get boots on the ground you will discover what we found: there are many other trails out here that are closed that we need to get reopened. We also hope you will treat them like you're an honored guest being treated to something special.

The first trail in this guidebook is a pass that climbs through the Caribou-Targhee National Forest to the top of the Lemhi mountain range. We started from the eastern side of this range on Spring Mountain Road, and right before the trail makes its steepest ascent to the top of the mountain, there is a parcel of private property that blocks an additional route.

I hiked around the perimeter of the property to document the condition of the closed public road that comes out of the back of the property, and I found the road was well maintained. This road accesses a high-altitude basin that contains numerous historic mining sites. There is also a series of switchbacks that scale a steep, exposed mountain to an amazing viewpoint of the Lemhi Range. It is the kind of trail that could sustain a small recreation culture of its own—think of it as Idaho's version of Black Bear Pass.

While there is an alternate route to get to the top of this mountain, opening this road would allow for the creation of a challenging loop along with access to the historic mining sites. After this field visit we've been reaching out to the Forest Service to petition them to open the road.

We continued our journey up and over the mountain, and it was a great mix of off-road technical challenge and breathtaking scenery. Traveling the trail took most of the day, and finishing the trail yielded the sense of accomplishment that comes from successfully navigating a challenge. As we descended the southern face and dropped below the tree line, we passed by some great dispersed camping areas.

This was a trail that checked a lot of the boxes for what we look for in the trail. I don't believe the trail is at immediate risk of closure, but the closed access into Horseshoe Gulch suggests that at some point in the recent past there was a trail with high recreation value that didn't have a passionate community willing to go the distance to fight to keep it open. Now that we know about it, we won't give up on getting the trail reopened, but preventing additional closures in an area like this which has already seen high value trails closed is why we create these guidebooks.

Each trail in this guidebook has its own story, and its own justification for our fight to keep them open. But this is something that you can only truly learn by experiencing your public lands for yourself.

Defend Your Ground,

Executive Director
BlueRibbon Coalition

Hidden Lemhi
Spring Mountain, ID

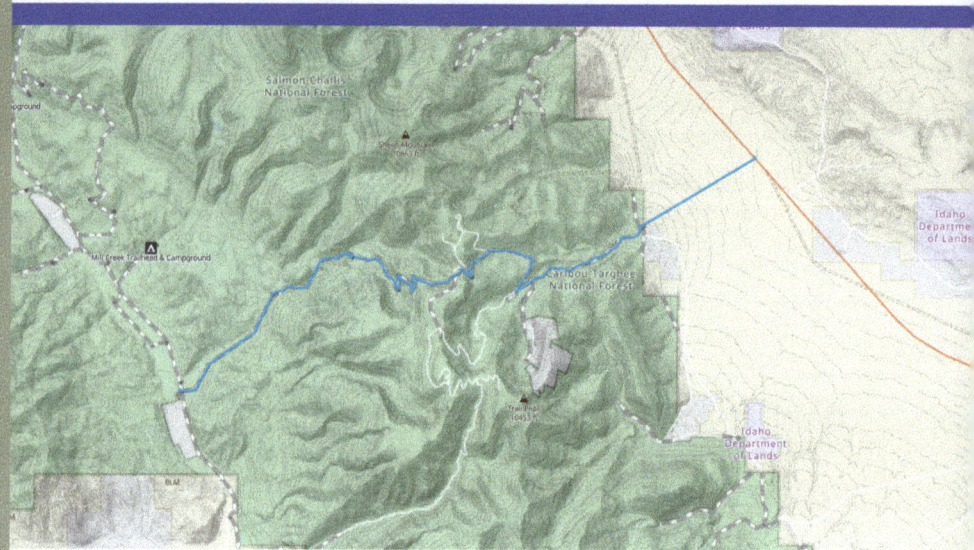

The Lemhi Mountain Range is one of Eastern Idaho's uniquely stunning landscapes. Sandwiched between the Beaverhead Range and the Lost River Range. The range stretches for almost 100 miles and contains Diamond Peak. Diamond Peak soars to 12,202 feet and is Idaho's third tallest mountain.

Numerous roads and trails provide access into the foothills and side canyons of Lemhi's formidable peaks, but if you really want to explore into the high country of these mountains, the Hidden Lemhi Pass is the premier route in this range.

If you're coming in from the north, you will leave the pavement of Highway 28 at Spring Mountain Road. The initial road is well graded and maintained until you get to a parcel of private property where the property owner is building a large cabin. At this point the road makes a switchback, and you will start to encounter more aggressive terrain.

From this point you will want to air down your tires, have high clearance, and four low.

The extra challenge from the terrain is worth it. Take your time and enjoy the high alpine scenery as you climb to the top of one of the range's highest passes. Expect shelf roads, lots of rocks, and a panoramic view from the top of three major mountain ranges that contain some of Idaho's highest mountains.

The descent is consistently challenging and provides additional opportunities to enjoy this rugged trail. The south side of the trail contains numerous great dispersed camping opportunities, and access routes into the Lost River Range or graded and paved roads that can get you back to the civilization of Idaho Falls.

Breathtaking open country near Spring Mountain on the Lemhi trail.

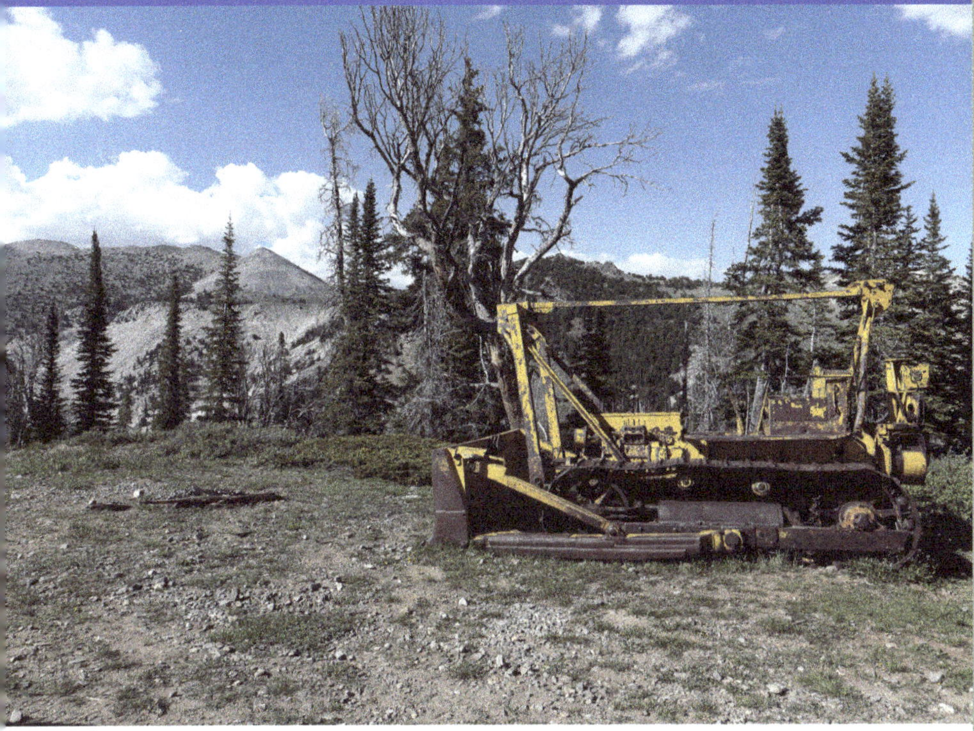

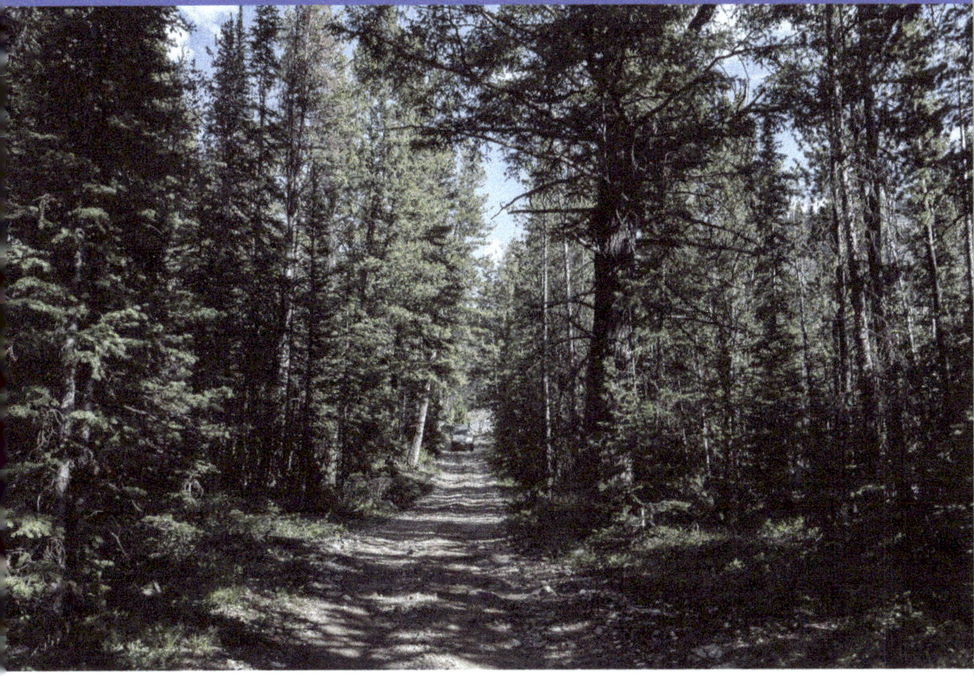

TRAIL SCOUTING & DOCUMENTATION
CONTRIBUTED BY

IDAHO STATE
4x4
ASSOCIATION

WWW.ID4X4A.COM

Bighole Mountain
South Horseshoe

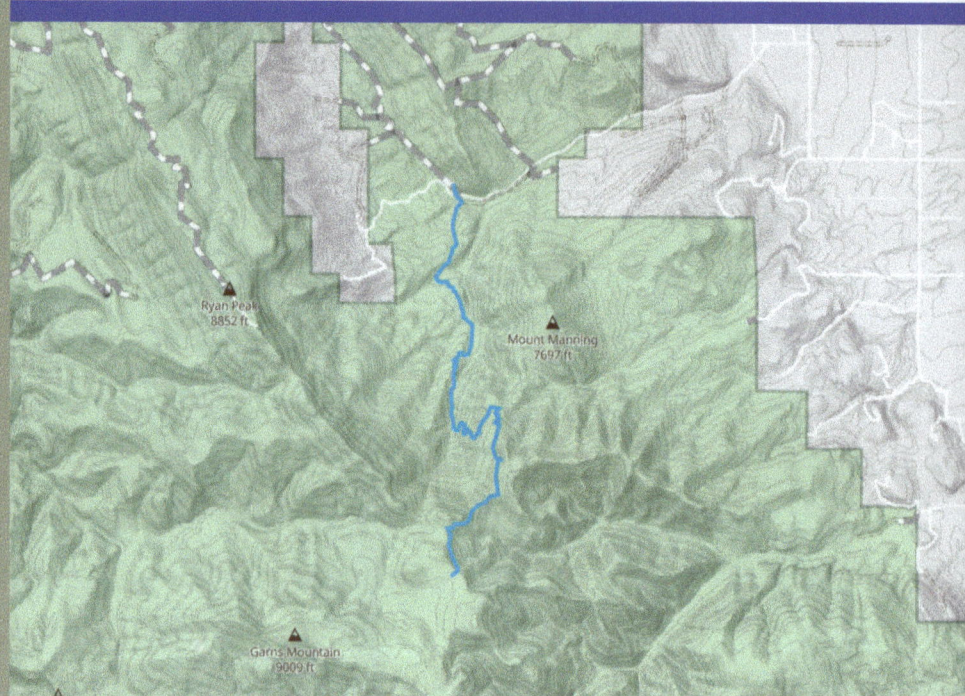

As E-bikes have gained in popularity, we have started to focus a small portion of our advocacy work on getting land managers to approve E-bike use on multiple-use, single track trails. During one of our trail inventory excursions, we called up our friends at Advocates for Multi-Use of Public Lands to see if they would have any interest in being part of this guidebook.

Their Executive Director, Will Mook, and our Executive Director, Ben Burr, decided to take their E-bikes for a spin in the Big Hole Mountains located between Driggs and Rexburg.

AMPL is a great group of advocates local to this area, and Will led the way up South Horseshoe. This popular dirtbike route is also used as a challenging E-bike route. It offers steep climbs through lush alpine forests, and when you stop to catch your breath, you can usually catch a nice view of the west face of the Tetons.

As a popular dirt-bike trail, this route was a decent challenge even on an E-bike. This is why we discussed ways we can also get E-bikes allowed on other U.S. Forest Service trails. Currently, public lands managers from the Bureau of Land Management, the National Park Service, and the U.S. Forest Service all treat E-bikes differently. The USFS is the most restrictive.

BRC is working with groups in Idaho to get legislation introduced and passed that would treat pedal-assist E-bikes like

other mountain bikes on trails located on federal lands. This would be a huge step forward for this growing new user group.

Meanwhile, if you're looking for a great destination for a summer single-track excursion, the Big Hole Mountains have a lot of great trails.

One of the e-bike trails coming through the Bighole Mountain route.

Blackrock Canyon
Pocatello, ID

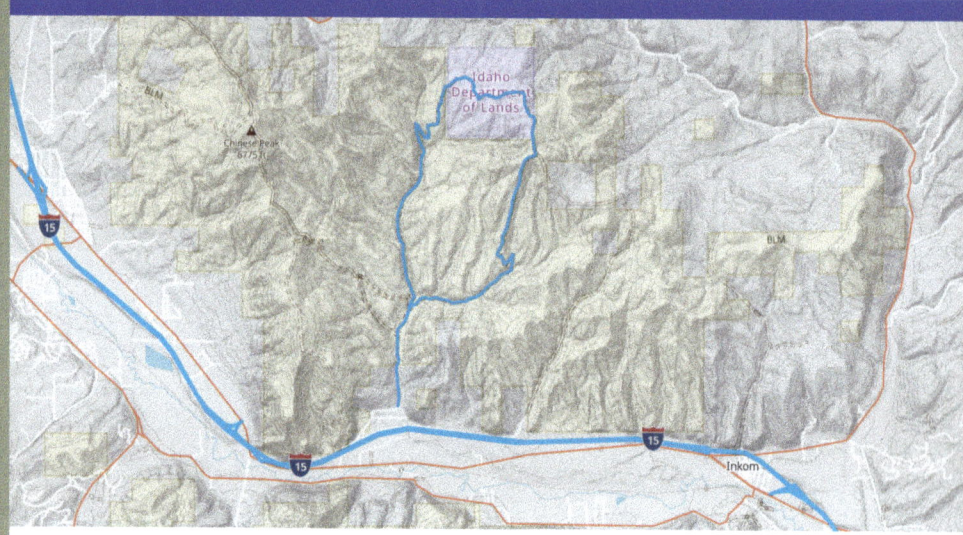

The Blackrock Canyon is a jewel of Pocatello that allows access to virtually all modalities of recreation. This area is home to some great single track hills, spectacular views, and a wide variety of full size roads allowing you to explore a large chunk of Bannock Range. For the 50" width trails, the trail length is over 60 miles of access and connects to Caddy Canyon.

Keeping all these trails open when the TMP comes along will be a challenge; showing that there is too much access breeds contempt with environmental groups. The BLM often sees it as an unnecessary need to have so many options. If you have been on these trails, you would think otherwise, and know that not running over a hiker when coming over a blind hill is probably a good thing!

These trails have so much diversity; it is really a great place. Some technical areas require low range for full size rigs, but that is about the only requirement. They are very scenic and allow you to get to some amazing dispursed camping areas. There are even a few spots along the trails with fire rings set up for public use. Please help keep these trails clean by practicing "Leave no trace."

BLM routes 301, 302, 113, 319, 351, 324

Coordinates: 42.8057, -112.3304

Length: 35 mi

Difficulty: 2

Trail Type: Suitable for all modalities

Getting there: If you are looking for trails in Pocatello this is your best set hands down. Iwould recommend coming in from the Chinese Peak side here at 42.84879, -112.36274 route 301, from here you drop down behind the radio towers. The back side of the towers are very steep, with loose sharp rock. On the easier access point at 42.81454, -112.33048 exit Old Hwy 91 off south bound I15 in Pocatello. Then take a left on N Blackrock Canyon Rd, this will take you to multiple parking lots and places to air down.

The stunning views from Blackrock Canyon make it an excellent weekend drive.

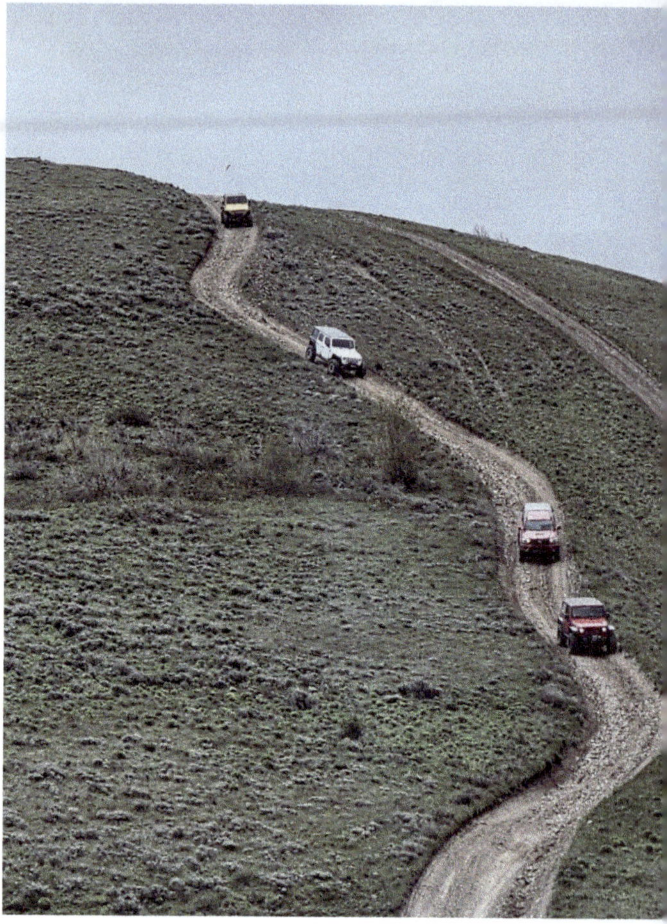

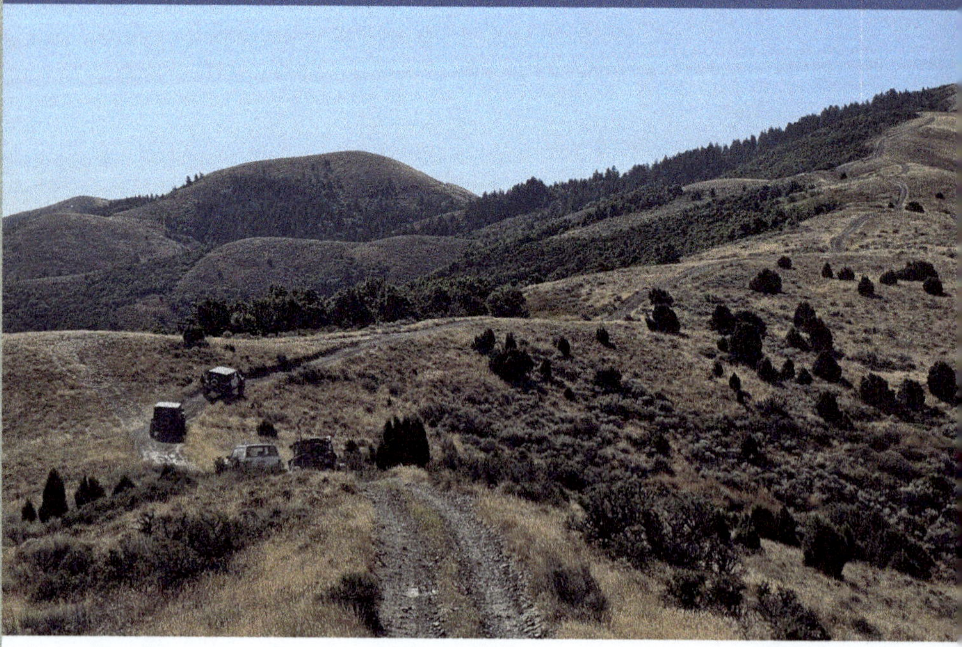

Chinese Peak
Pocatello, ID

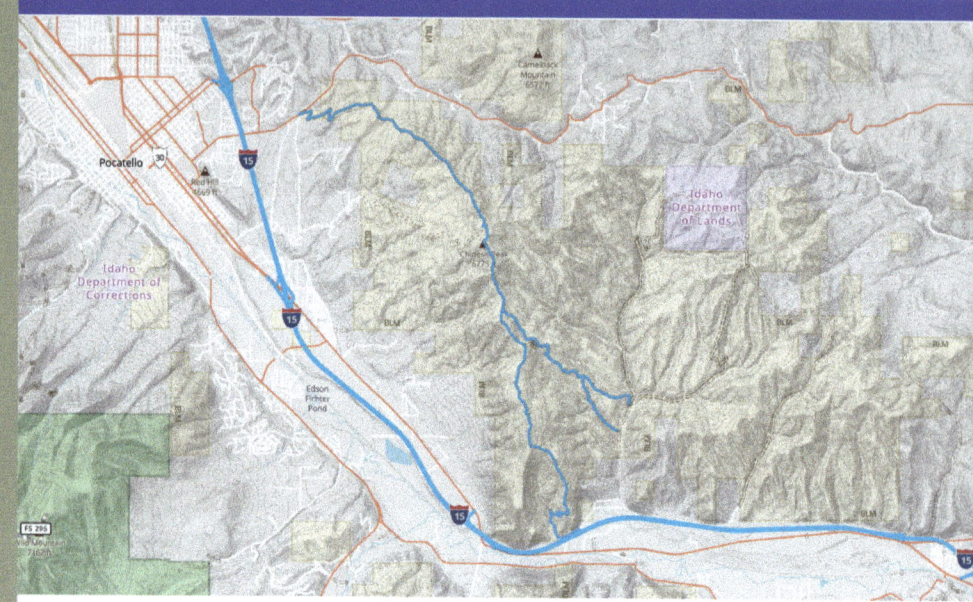

There are several ways to approach the radio towers on the top of Chinese Peak—two that are wild and one that is mild. The standard road up to the top is off of Barton road and turns into route 301. This way can be a little nerve-wracking because of loose gravel and constant switch backs but not difficult in the least. This is an access road for utility use, as well as general use for sightseeing.

The north and south routes however are a different story. On the north, route 352 begins at a multi-use trail head. This route is popular with single track and cross country running. As you work your way up the hill, there are several steep ascents with multiple offshoots of the trail to add to the difficulty. Loose sharp rocks will keep you thinking. Four low and a good seatbelt is needed. These trails will undoubtedly become under fire with upcoming TMP's. With multiple points of access their excuse would likely be redundant roads for entry to an overused area, though it was developed for this specific purpose.

The south side of the trail has numerous drop offs that will make your heart skip a beat. Going up the peak is even more exhilarating. The trails are open to all motorized and even have a few sections that are for under 50" and motorcycle specific. The southern side enters from the Blackrock Canyon route 3110, the track will run you down the mountain through multiple groves manicured into tight tunnels. Numerous dispersed camp sites are scattered down the mountain side all the way to the canyon floor.

Trail Guide: BLM Route 352

Coordinates: 42.87080, -112.40682

Length: 3mi

Difficulty:2

Trail Type: All Motorized

Take the S 5th St exit off Hwy 15 in Pocatello, back track to Barton Rd, and take a Right. You can continue up Barton till the utility service trail head. (But, that is not much fun!) Take a left under the Hwy 15 overpass on American Rd. This will dead end to East Terry, and the air down spot is directly to the right at 42.87080, -112.40682.

A line of adventurers follows the road to the radio tower, following the Chinese Peak trail.

Craters of the Moon
Arco, ID

The Craters of the Moon is a side by side travelers dream trail hands down at just around seventy five miles. There is nothing that is overly difficult on this trail unless it has been raining and you find a rut. If you do please use your best judgement in proceeding and not destroying the trail. The scenic views are the main draw to this area. While it may seem like a big flat desert this loop shows some of the amazing qualities that Idaho has to offer.

There is a vast trail system out in this area that has been used for hunting and recreation for decades. This chosen path will take you on the outskirts of the Craters of the Moon National Monument and Great Rift wilderness study area. A hot topic lately has been an expansion of these wilderness areas to "preserve" the area. They are calling them buffer zones. This would eliminate why this trail is specifically amazing.

Depending on the time of year you will come across herds of Elk and Pronghorn, even Moose if it is later in the winter season. With the large number of trails in the vicinity, there will surely be attempts to close off roads that are "untraveled". Calling these trails untraveled is misleading because some roads function as alternate routes to prevent resource damage.

Getting there: The beginning of the trail begins around 43.44175, -112.80814 out of Arco at the crossing of Big Butte Rd and Main to 26. South on Tabler road that turns into Atomic City to Frenchman's Cabin, and the land starts to get desolate. As you follow along you come to the split of Cedar Big Butte and Moms Cox Well; whichever way you choose the result is the same as it is one large loop.

Trail Guide: BLM, Craters of the Moon

Coordinates: 43.4192, -112.8999

Length: 75 miles

Difficulty: 1

Trail Type: All modalities (popular for SXS)

The open trail near Craters of the Moon.

FIND ADVENTURE
SUPPORT ACCESS

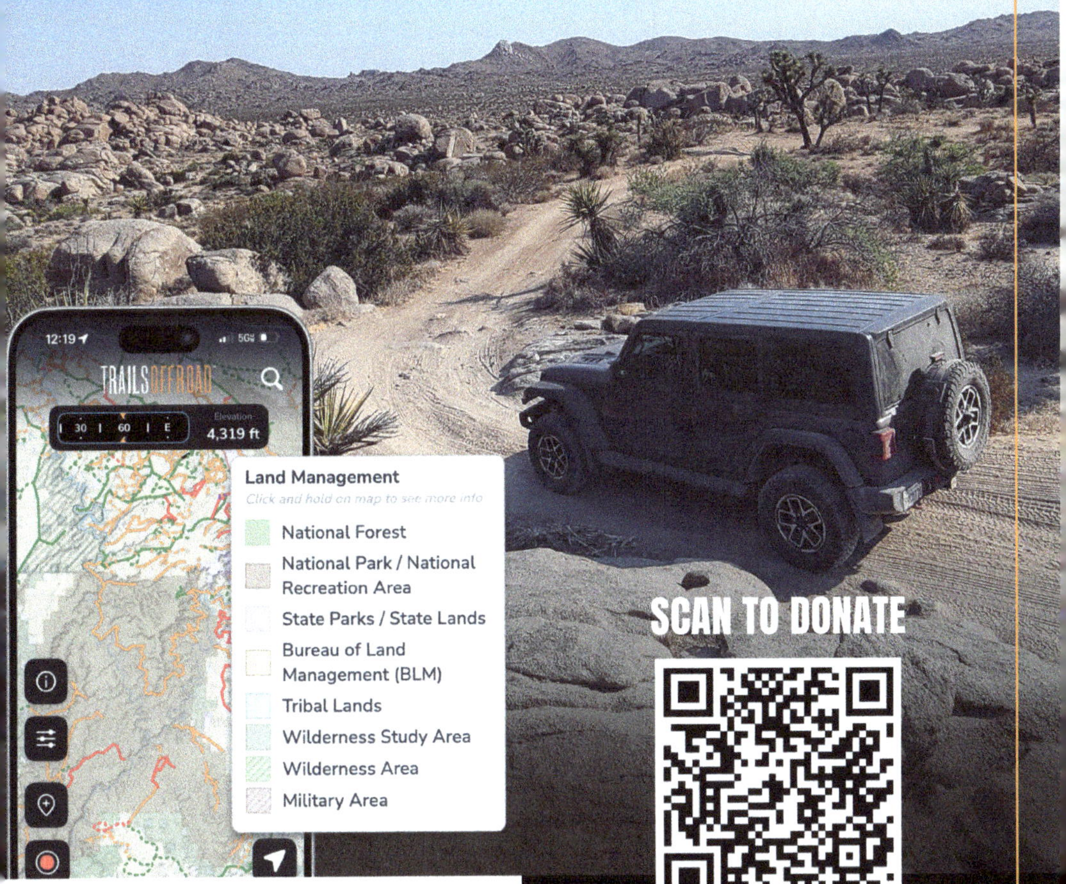

Land Management
Click and hold on map to see more info

- National Forest
- National Park / National Recreation Area
- State Parks / State Lands
- Bureau of Land Management (BLM)
- Tribal Lands
- Wilderness Study Area
- Wilderness Area
- Military Area

SCAN TO DONATE

1 **SCAN THE QR CODE** TO GO **ALL-ACCESS** ON TRAILS OFFROAD™

2 40% OF YOUR UPGRADE GETS DONATED DIRECTLY TO BRC

3 DOWNLOAD THE MOBILE APP AND FIND YOUR NEXT FAVORITE TRAIL

TRAILSOFFROAD™

Member trail reviews on Trails Offroad™ are an invaluable resource the BRC can utilize to *Defend Our Ground* in the fight against trail closures across the country. Adventure and offroad advocacy go hand-in-hand with a **Trails Offroad™ All-Access Membership.**

Dairy Lake
Leadore, ID

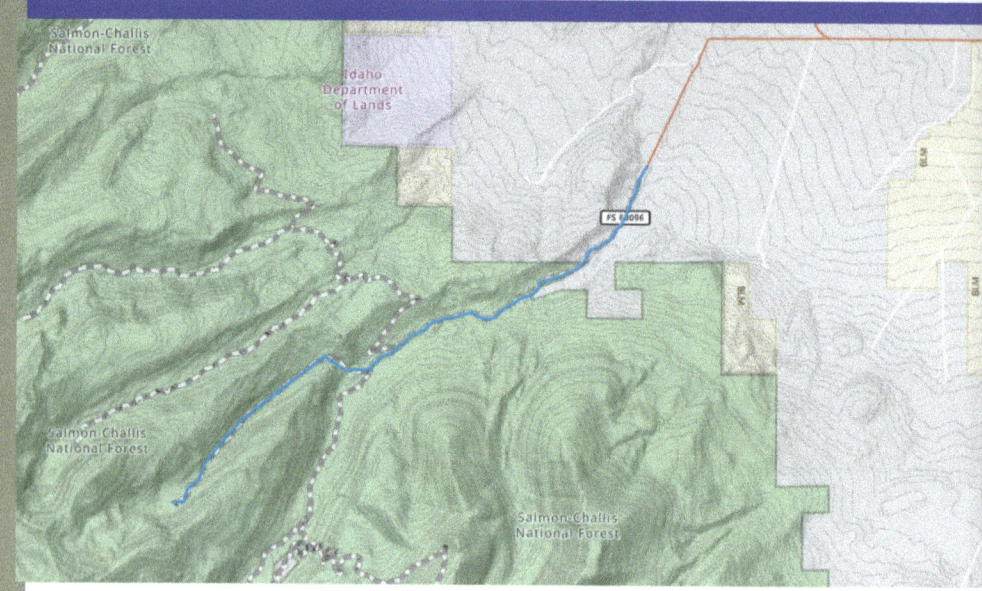

Just outside of Leadore, at coordinates 44.63623, 113.55522 you will find an excellent group of trails and lakes. The Snake River Offroaders affectionately call these trails the Three Lakes, it even has a fourth wonder that is rarely explored. East to West if you are up for it all three trails could be done in one long day with a small group. Dairy Lake is a wonderful trail to break your teeth on and test out that new rig. The SXS community absolutely loves this trail, as well, providing a steady flow of traffic through a town that needs every dollar.

A modest trail rated at a 1 to 2, passable by any vehicle with decent clearance and 4x4. Dairy Lake has a gatekeeper of medium sized loose rocks leading to a water crossing with a bridge that may or may not be in operational condition. After the bridge it will be a delightful trail full of bumps and ledges. If you are lucky all the trees from the seasonal fell will have been removed, but we would be prepared to break out the saw. If you are in a small group, this trail can be done in a little over an hour.

When you get to the top the view is absolutely stunning. The water in the lake comes from a snow pack and is not stocked, but there are fish lurking. This is an invaluable hunting area to elk hunters for generations. If on foot there are several flat areas you can camp around the lake, but overlanding is difficult as there is very little accessible beach that is not on an incline. These types of trails are an endangered species and must be protected for use by all and looked at when the Forest Service begins their planning processes.

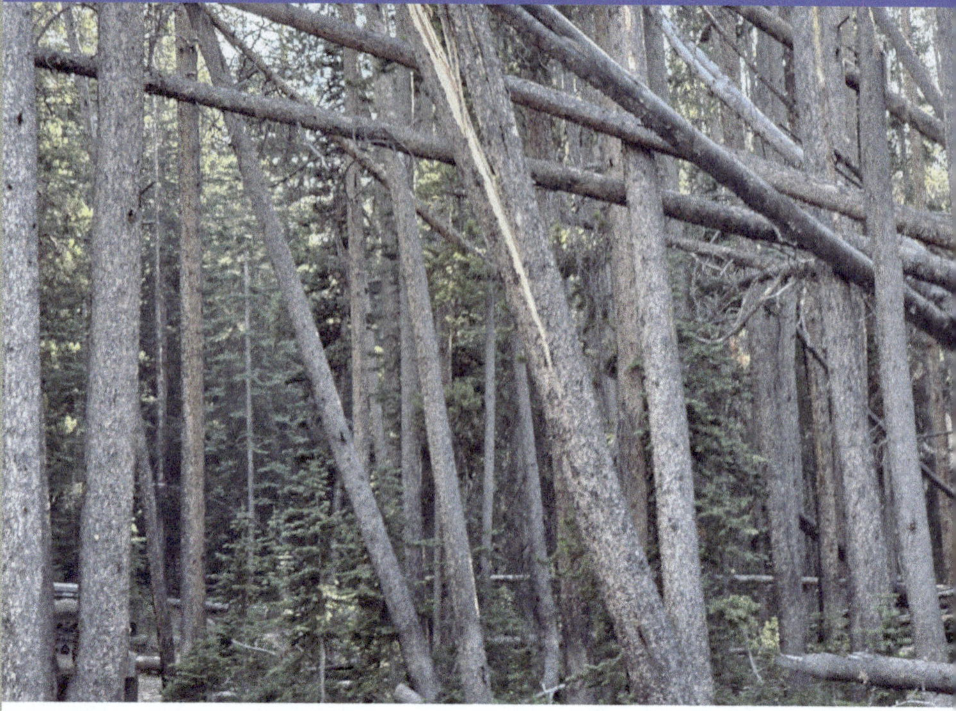

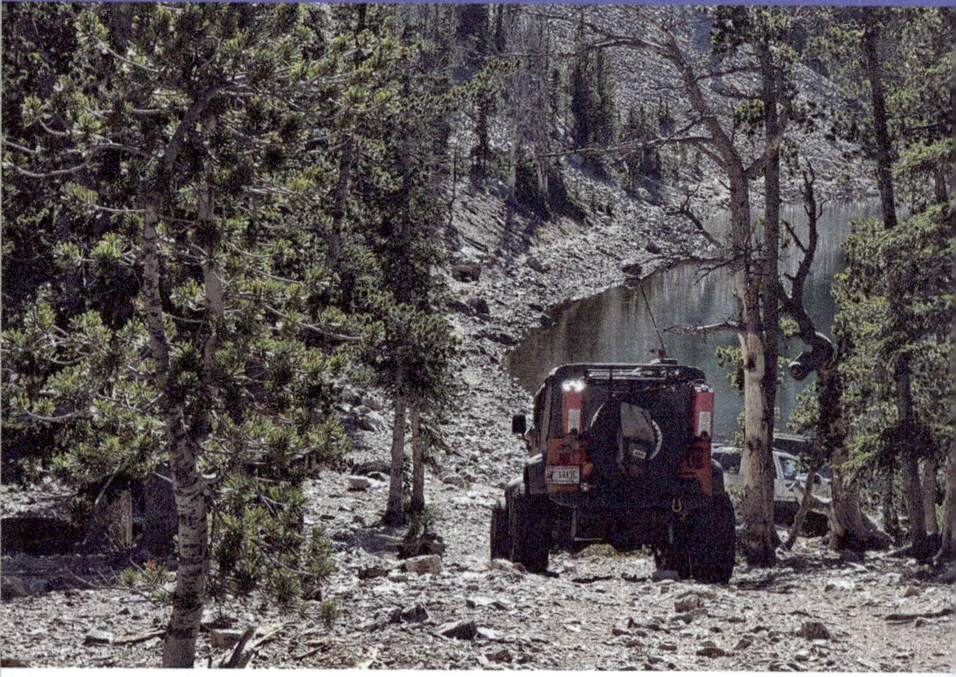

Trail: NFS Route 6004, Dairy Lake

Coordinates: 44.63623, -113.55522

Length: 5 Mi

Difficulty: 2

Trail Type: Suitable for all modalities (SXS, Full-Sized, etc.)

Getting there: Go West out of Leadore on Lee Cr to Big Eight Mile Rd and turn left. Make sure to stay left and continue slowly for a few miles through a few sections of private property. The turn offs for all the 3 Lakes trails are clearly marked. Dairy Creek Trail #6004 starts at coordinates 44.19979, -113.83285. The very back of Eight Mile Rd is Eight Mile Camp ground.

Deep Creek
Rockland, ID

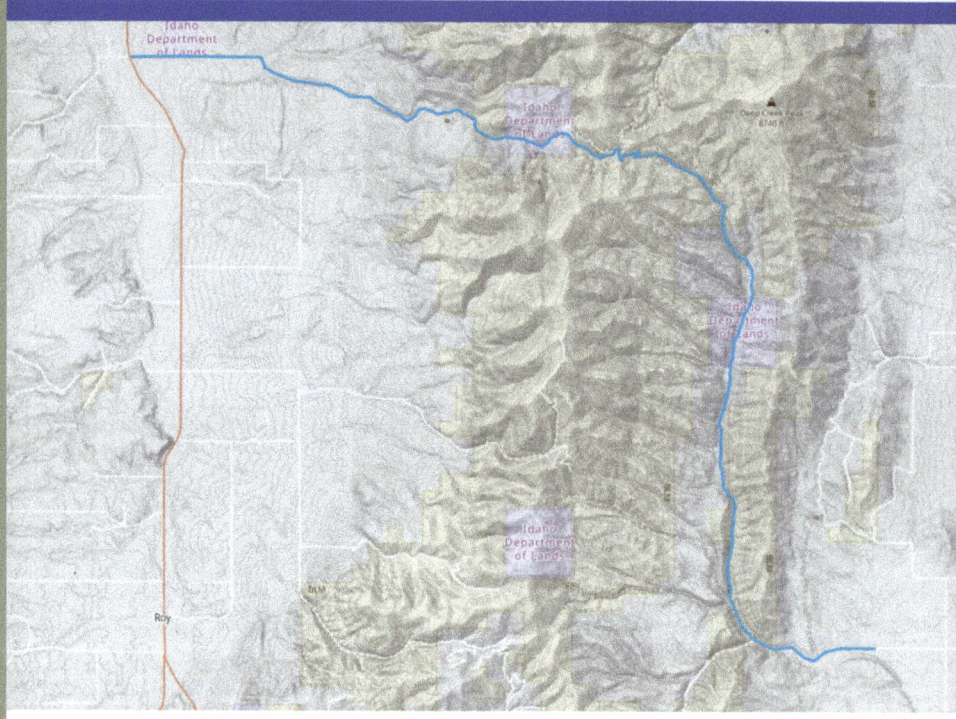

Deep Creek has a vast trail system, spurred from old logging roads, that stretches well over a hundred miles. Any offshoot you take will lead you to a deep wooded wonder or a sprawling scenic view. In the past this was a very well-developed forest logging area and the lack of travel is evident. The main roads take minimal maintenance due to the lack of activity and the trail proper is remarkably gentle. If you look hard enough, you will find some rough areas that are too hard to get to with the machinery, so it makes for some fun, rutty goodness!

The lack of use is a concern to many that follow closures. The thinking being that the lack of use will get the offshoots closed down to reclaim. The obscure location is not going to help matters much, either, since it is nestled between Burley and Pocatello, which offers minimal travel and even less recreation other than some spectacular hunting. That just means that it is a perfect opportunity to make it a destination off-roading adventure area! Which the Idaho State 4x4 Association is looking to achieve.

There are multiple loops within this area and you are no way limited to a particular trail or road. It is a large area that you should most certainly explore, each just as beautiful as the last. We highly suggest wandering!

Getting There: Depending on which way you are coming from, this area is easily accessible. From American Falls you will come in on State Hwy 37 South through Rockland, then go East on Knox Canyon Rd. If you are coming in from the east, the southern side entrance to the area is very beautiful. Coming in from any direction, take the Bull Canyon Rd. It runs North directly up the Bull Canyon and is surrounded by lush greenery Spring and Summer and is engulfed in snow pack during the winter, making entry a great challenge.

Trail Guide: Deep Creek Mtns, BLM

Coordinates: 42.4803, -112.8409

Length: 30 mi

Difficulty: 1-2

Trail Type: Full Size, SXS, Dirt Bike

The quiet hills, bristly fir trees, and tall grasses waiting on the Deep Creek trail.

REXBURG
MOTORSPORTS
RZR
PRO
ALES - PARTS - SERVICE - GEAR - APPAREL
WWW.REXBURGMOTORSPORTS.COM
(208) 356-4000

Diamond Peak
Lemhi Range, ID

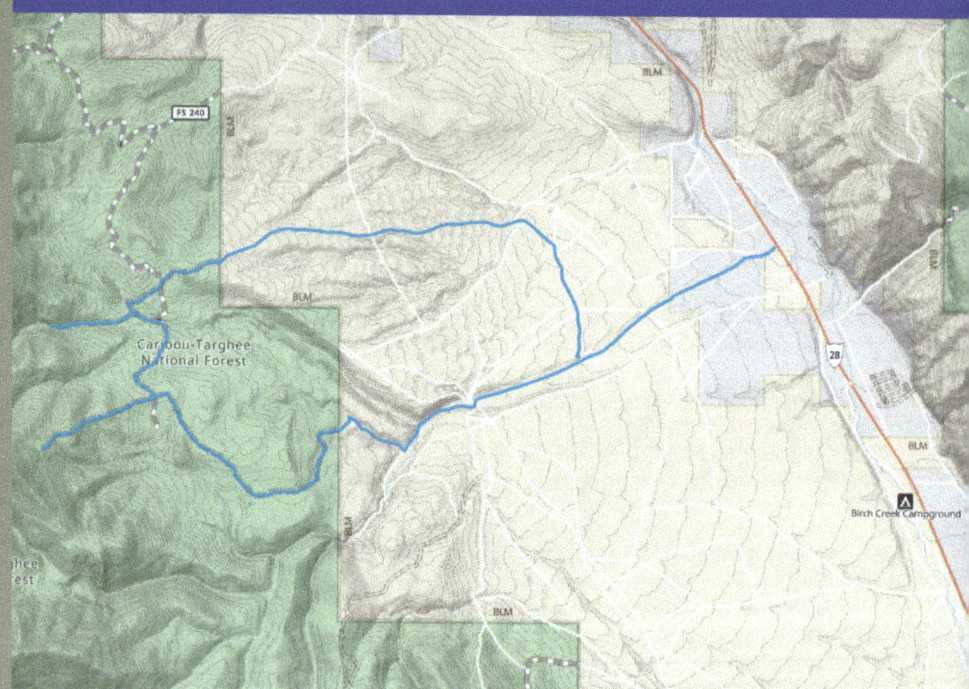

Diamond Peak is the third highest peak in Idaho, and the highest mountain in the Lemhi range. At 12,202 feet, it is a popular destination for hikers. This popular hiking trail is also a great example of how motorized trails make non-motorized recreation possible. The trailhead to start this hike is at the end of a pretty rugged backcountry trail.

While the trail itself isn't difficult, the last 500 feet to the hiking trailhead take you straight up a mountain. The views along the trail make the drive worth the trek even if you're not planning to hike to the top of Diamond Peak.

While we regularly hear from non-motorized users that closing trails is justified because people can still "just walk" to enjoy these trails, we observed that no one was starting the hike to the top of Diamond Peak from the valley floor. Everyone was using motorized 4x4 vehicles to ascend the first 2,000 feet in elevation gain to start their hike several miles closer to the summit at around 8,000' feet.

While we were exploring this area, we noticed another spur route that explored another draw coming off the northeast face of Diamond Peak. We had a hunch that there would be an epic dispersed campsite at the end of this spur, and after exploring the route, we can confirm that the campsite at the end of FS 753 is a hidden gem.

Spurs like this that are located near a popular hiking trailhead are often closed, because the high elevation mountain ranges are often targets for wilderness designations. If the Lemhi range were to ever be designated as wilderness, it is likely a route to the trailhead would be cherry-stemmed into the wilderness, but we would almost certainly lose access to the unnamed spur routes like FS 753. There are numerous spur routes like this up and down this range, and we encourage you to go out and explore these routes.

Trail Guide: Diamond Peak/ FS 796, Kaufman Springs/ FS 35, Diamond Peak #2/ FS 753

Coordinates: 44.1449, -112.984

Length: 16.4 miles

Difficulty: 1

Trail Type: All modalities

The tranquil woods along the trail at Diamond Peak, an offroad adventure for all modalities.

East Fork to Crestline
Pocatello, ID

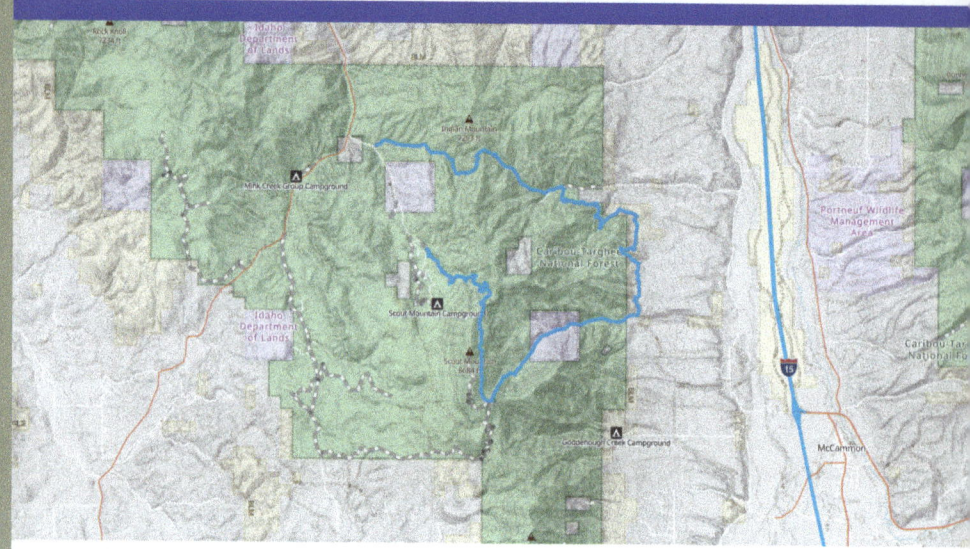

This loop offers both challenges and rewards for the adventurous. This loop wraps around Scout Mountain, offering technical uphills with root and rock sections, exposed traverse sections, and a fun descent back to the starting point. You'll also be rewarded with meadows carpeted with springtime flowers, and commanding views of the surrounding Portneuf area.

From the bottom, head up South Mink Creek Road (FS 001) to the campground at the top. As you climb East Fork, you'll reach a meadow that offers a good place to stop and snack, take pictures, and enjoy the scenery. Then as you keep traveling, the trail passes by a pond that occasionally hosts the local moose before reaching the crux of the climb. This next section is steep and rocky with several switchbacks, climbing continuously until it reaches Scout Mountain Top Road. Take a left and climb up the gravel road to roughly the six mile point, then look for a singletrack trail dropping to the right with a sign for Crestline trail. The first section traverses the east face of Scout Mountain, and is exposed with a drop to your right. Once you reach the high point of the trail, it will drop down to a lookout overlooking the Portneuf Gap. This is another great spot to take a break and take in the scenery.

All that's left at this point is the descent back to the parking lot, traveling through the trees. Keep an eye out for uphill hiking traffic, especially on the weekends, as this is a popular climb.

East Fork is the keystone of the whole Scout Mountain trail system, connecting to Blind Spring Draw, Valve House, Box

Spring, Crestline, and others. Crestline is a popular day hike, and provides access all the way to the summit of Scout Mountain There is a connector from the bottom of Crestline over to Lead Draw that has already had access curtailed recently due to interference with a public shooting range.

Getting there: from Mink Creek Rd, turn south on FS road 00 and travel 3 miles, and look for a left turn marked Crestline Trailhead. This spot can be popular on weekends and holidays, so it's a good idea to get there early. This loop typically doesn't open up til around Memorial Day due to snow.

Trail Guide: East Fork Mink Creek/Crestline Loop

Coordinates: 42.7070500, -112.3624100

Length:11.4 miles

Difficulty: moderate

Trail Type: suitable for hiking, motorcycles, mountain bikes

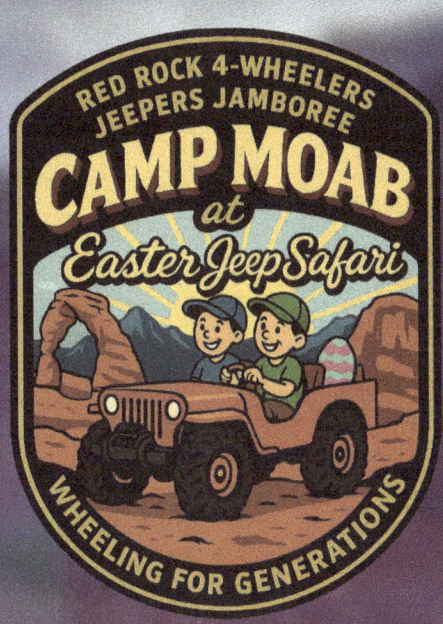

YOUR HOSTS FOR

Easter Jeep Safari, Camp Moab at EJS, Labor Day Camp Out & Trail of the Month Series

The premier off-road club focused on family fun 4-wheeling, responsible recreation & public land stewardship.

facebook.com/redrock4wheelers
youtube.com/@rr4wmoab

www.RR4W.com
435-259-ROCK

Everson Lake
Leadore, ID

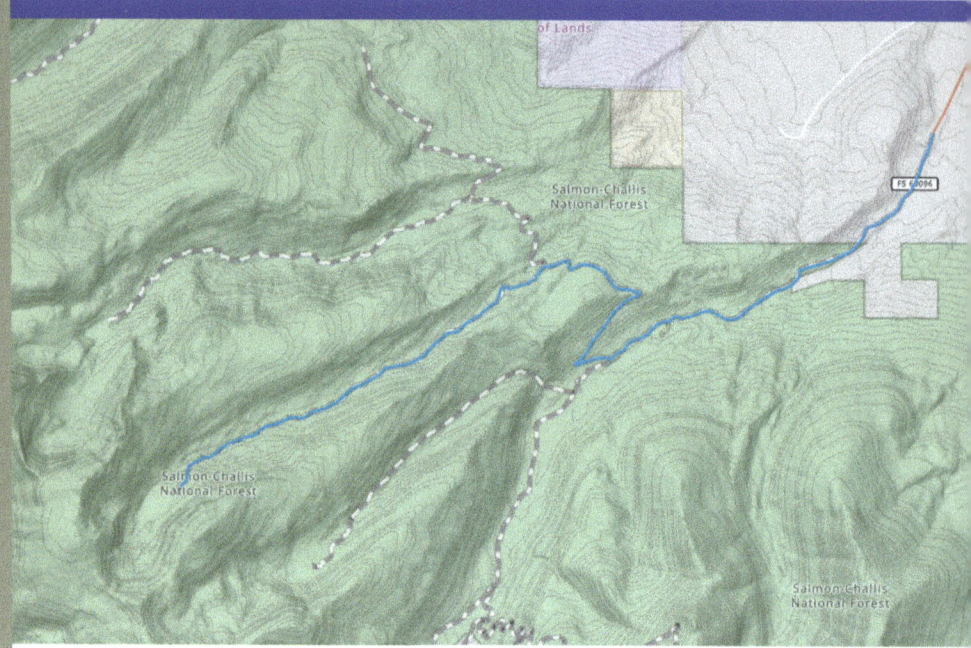

Continuing on the tour of Leadore deep in the Salmon National Forest is Everson Lake route #6006. Everson Lake is undoubtedly the easiest of the three lakes and can be done with virtually any vehicle and accessible for drivers of all skill levels. It is the longest of the three routes at close to two and a half hours depending on group size. Everson is absolutely stunning; it meanders gently through the picturesque landscapes.

Atop the trail you come to crystal clear waters that reflect the towering cliffs, cradling an epic backdrop. Everson and the trail itself are perfect spots for photography, picnics, or simply soaking in the serene environment, with lots of space to camp, as well. It is a perfect example of a leisurely alpine trail with a creek running nearly the entire length of the trail. On the way up, you come to a decrepit miner's cabin, half-standing, that dates back to the early 1900s. If on horse or foot, this would be the optimal trail in the area as it is not nearly as rough as the others locally.

These trails are a perfect example of the routes we need to protect. When it comes time to start closing trails, groups that wish to "preserve" love to target lonely lakes such as this. Never mind the fact that full size and SXS groups are the ones that maintain the area.

Getting there: Go West out of Leadore on Lee Cr to Big Eight Mile Rd and turn left. The coordinates for the turn off are 44.63989, -113.55000 to Everson and Stroud Cr the road is marked 64004. Spur left at the well-marked trailhead, Route 6006. Stay on designated paths to protect the natural environment. In the early season, watch for remaining snow and icy patches on the trail.

A look back along the Eversone Lake trail.

Trail Guide: FS Route 6006, Everson Lake

Coordinates: 44.63989, -113.55000

Length: 5.2 Mi

Difficulty: 1

Trail Type: Suitable for all modalities (SXS, Full-Sized, etc.)

BRINGING TOGTHER
THE VOICE OF THE

OFF-ROADING COMMUNITY
TO KEEP ROADS AND TRAILS OPEN

OVER 250 VENDORS
& 30,000 + ATTENDEES

SLOREX.COM

Hell's Half Acre
Shelley, ID

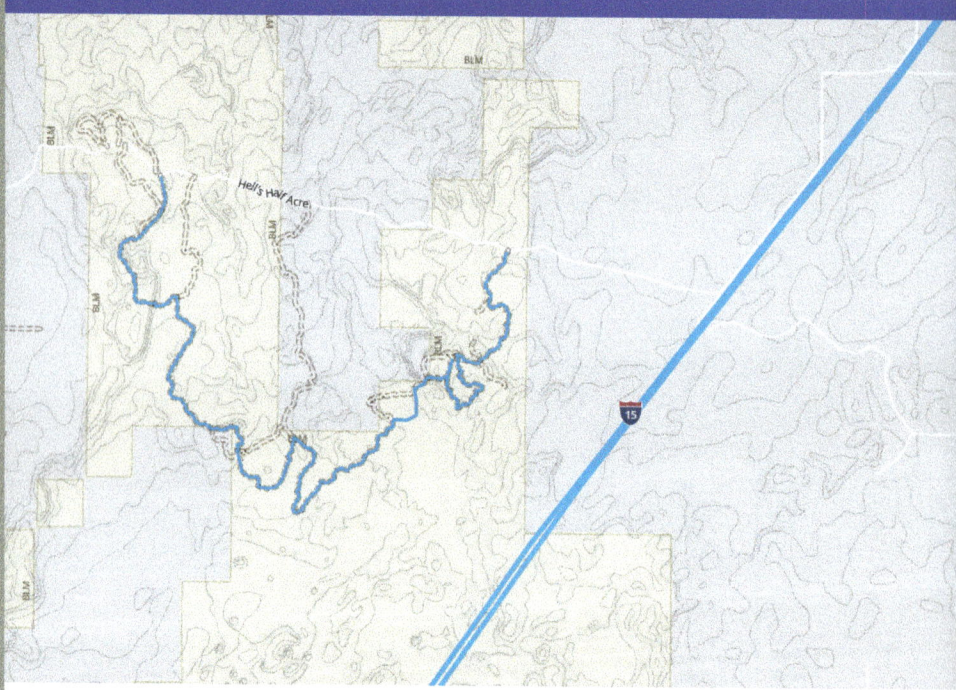

Hell's Half Acre is a particularly interesting set of trails that have some serious implications for the SE Idaho off road scene. Hell's has not been designated, though it has been used for decades by the local clubs for what is some of the most difficult wheeling in the area. The Snake River Off-Roaders are the stewards of the trail, doing multiple clean up efforts per year and ensuring everyone that comes for a challenge leaves impressed. The BLM in the near future will be looking at this area soon as more TMP's roll out.

These trails can be run in any direction and at any time of year, though we would suggest going with a guide and certainly not alone. Deep fissures and razor sharp ledges take great joy in destroying tires. The superb grip of the lava rock shatters axles and u-joints at nearly every outing. Any vehicle with low range and good clearance is fine—the bigger tires the better, as the cracks will swallow anything under 35s.

This patch of trails is nestled in between multiple private land sections and a mix of State and BML land. We feel these trails are highly susceptible to closure due to the logistics of getting there. Weaving through farm after farm and being so close to a wilderness study area makes keeping this open a necessity due to the propensity of BLM to create "buffer zones" around their coveted areas.

Getting there: Just west of Shelley Idaho take the Shelley Exit E 1250. Go West and take Horseshoe Rd South and zig zag down a bit to N 1000 aka Lava Rd. Wheelers normally air down and park trailers at the wide pull off south of the Lava Road about 1.2 miles from the east end of Lava Road. There are four access points for the trails. From east to west. The first is Quarry road, second is the Middle Road just past the agricultural fields, next is Cowards Way out and the fourth is the Meadow. Generally, we start a run at the Meadow access point. All will make for a great day!

Trail Guide: BLM Route undesignated

Coordinates: 43.3542, -112.2441

Length: 13mi

Difficulty: 4

Trail Type: Suitable for Full Size and SXS

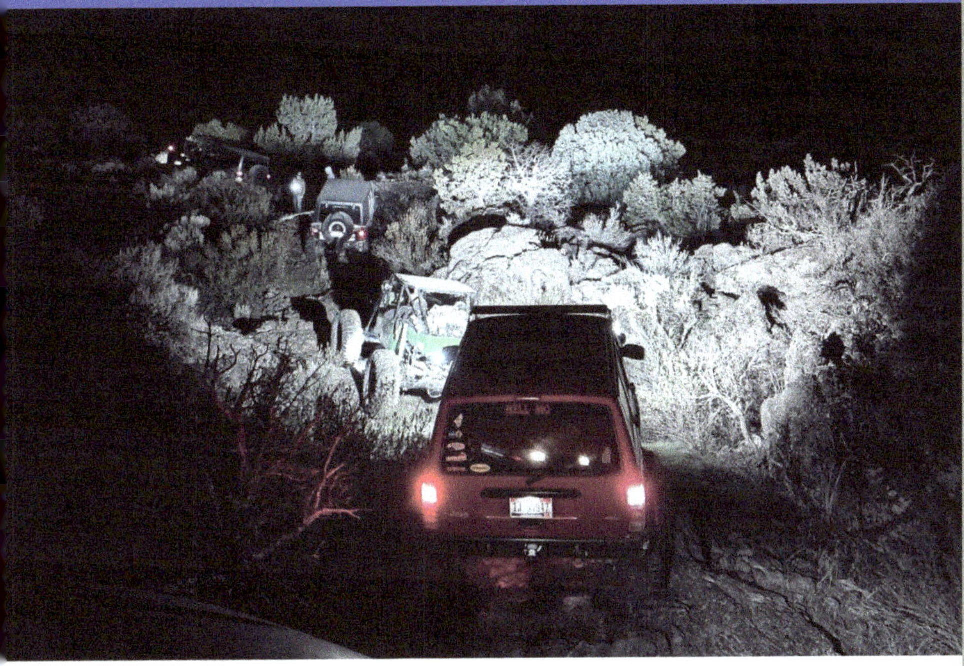

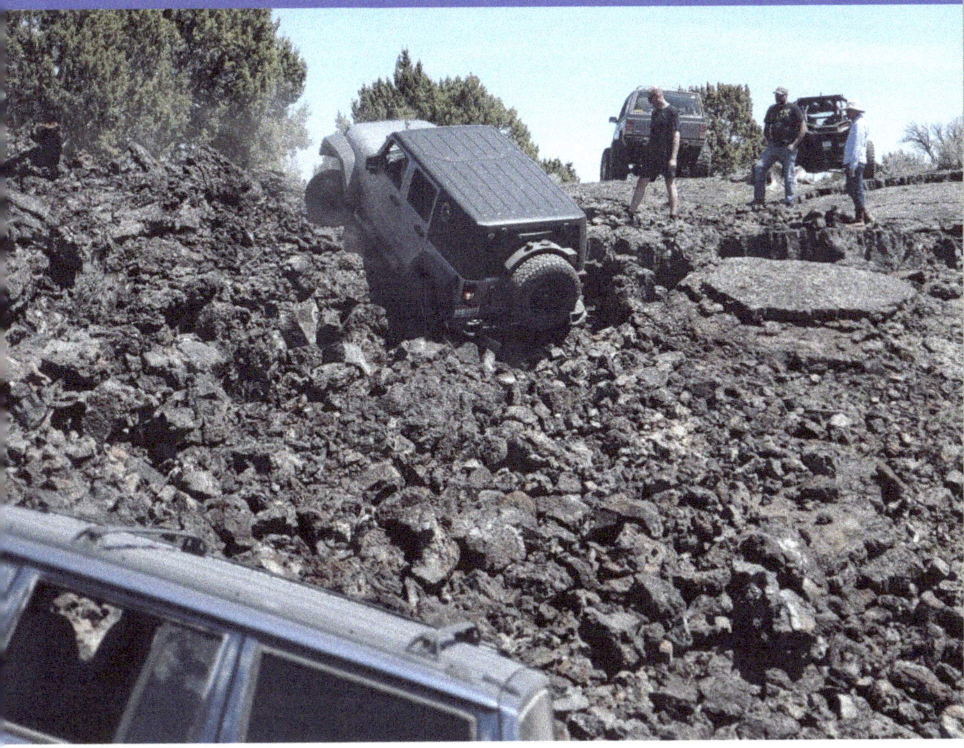

South East Idaho's Premier Off road club

No Road
No Problem

SNAKE RIVER OFFROADERS

Find us on Facebook and at
www.snakeriveroffroaders.org

Indian Creek to Rexbur

Bancroft, ID

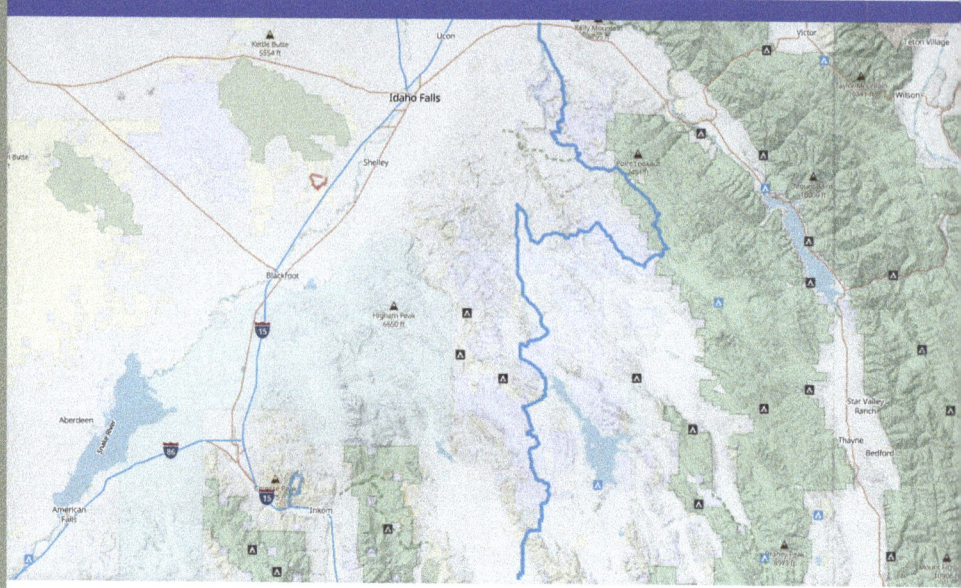

This route starts off just outside of Bancroft deep in the heart of farm country and heads north up and over Ten Mile Pass. You will drop down into cow heaven with green grass, water flows, and rarely traversed roads that are full of cattle. This makes a great beginning to the trail. Looking at the surrounding map, there are loads of options of directions to take and peaks to see. The Indian Creek Cow Camp winds through a large portion of Idaho Dept of Lands and over a few private tracks. You will see some amazing views that go on for days and even some of the logging efforts for the state.

After miles and miles of rustic trail through cattle country you will meet up with the Brush Creek Rd out of Wolverine around Smiley Canyon. This is a well-maintained county road, but leads to some amazing open spaces including some great dispersed camping areas. One of the best sits right off the Blackfoot River at 43.00048, -111.73017, with enough room for a dozen rigs. This road will wrap around and back up the East side of the Blackfoot Mountain Range bringing you up into Bone. Make sure you stop off at the Bone Store and show your support for a company that strongly supports outdoor rec of all modalities.

Coming out of Bone, work your way back down SE up, over and through Pine Mountain, seeing some spectacular greenery. This is an amazing area for a fall run, but beware of the wildlife.

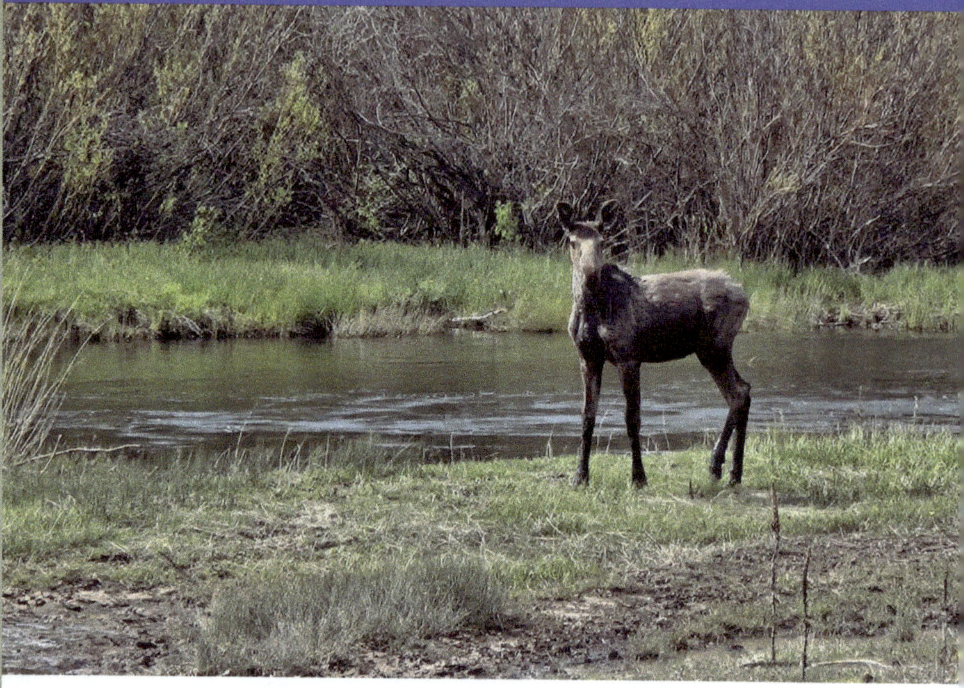

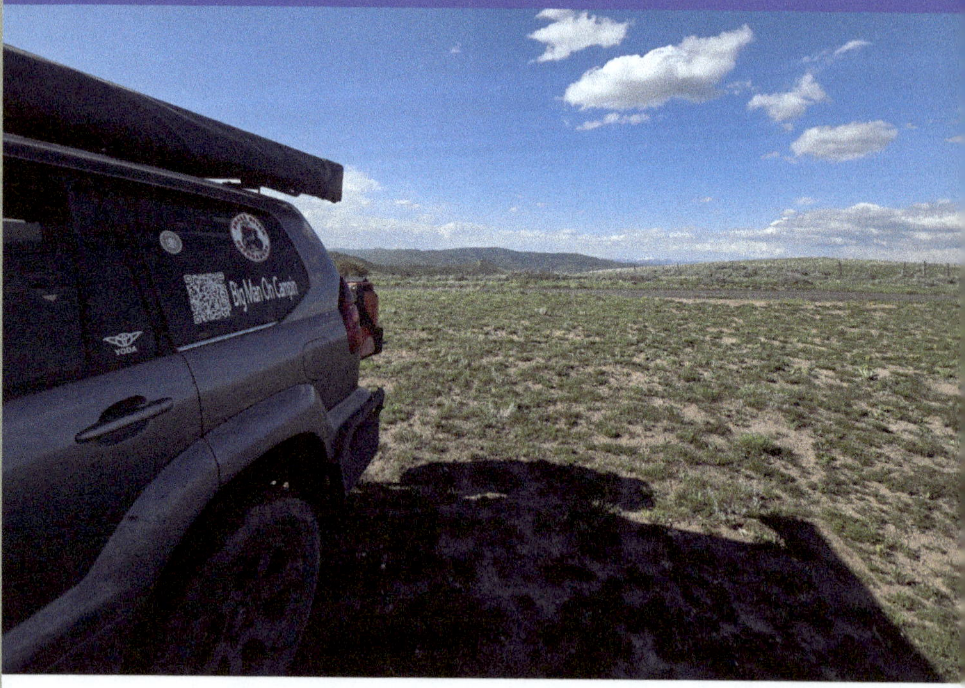
Big Man On Campin
YODA

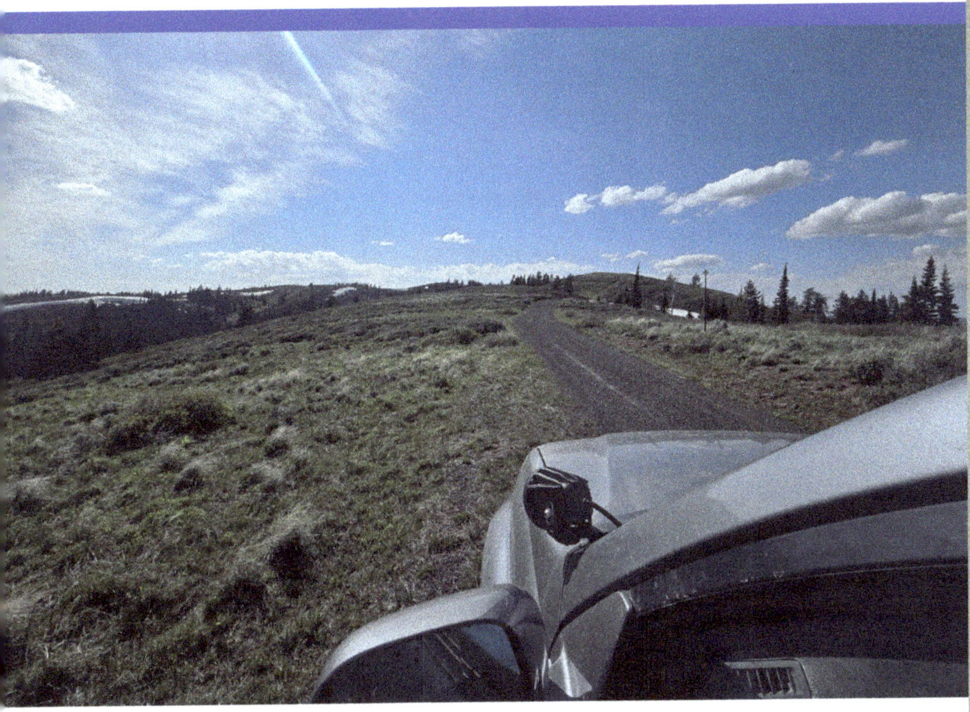

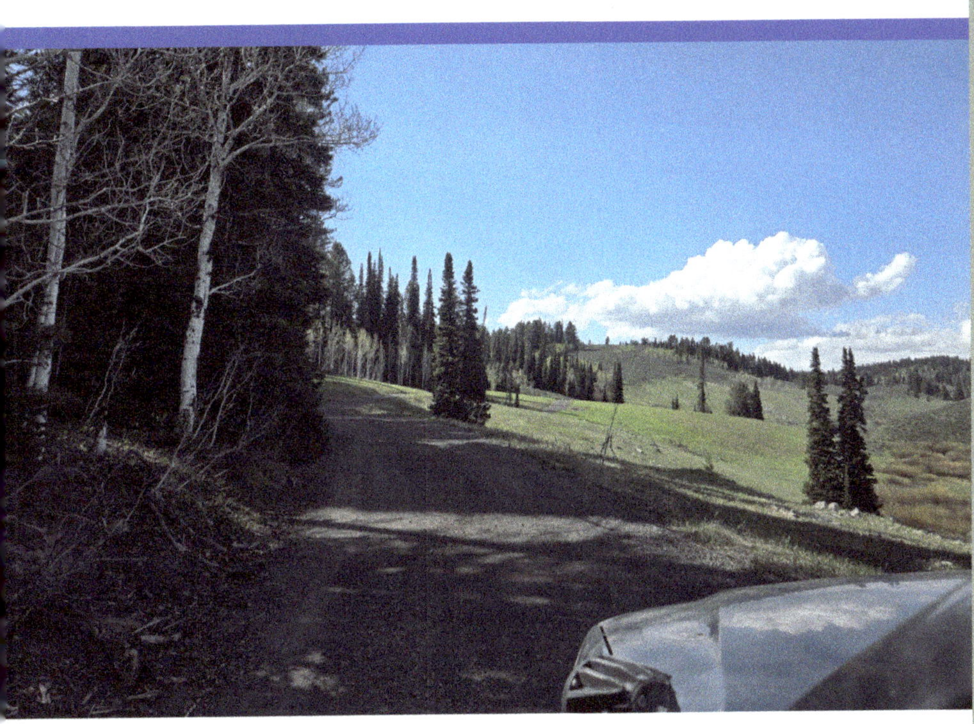

Moose and bear are prevalent in the area. This trail is very casual and scenic until you hit the Brockman Guard Station. At that point you will start your trek up Skyline Ridge 40075, over some rocky points and then come to a decision of whether you want to continue the easy route or hit June Creek 40376, which we highly recommend. June Creek is a local hot spot with some killer camping atop its ridge. The sunsets are stellar, and if you go at the right time of year, you may actually make it out! During the rainy season, this trail is very challenging. The modest hills that seemed like they have been greased can be a problem going up and down.

After you make it through the soup and out of the ruts, the path out is a nice, casual drive once more that winds through some really cool canyons. This trip is for someone that wants to be on a dirt road all day long and not have to worry about stoplights. The road will lead you all the way up into Ririe Reservoir. Here you can camp for the evening near the water and experience some pretty good fishing.

Getting There: You start off old Hwy 30 SE of Bancroft no matter which direction you come in from. Take Talmage Rd, North through a few zig zags to Rigby Rd North to the Tenmile Cutoff. Here begins your journey.

Trail Guide: Indian Creek to Ririe

Coordinates: 42.6846, -111.7892

Length: 144 mi

Difficulty: 1-2

Trail Type: All modalities

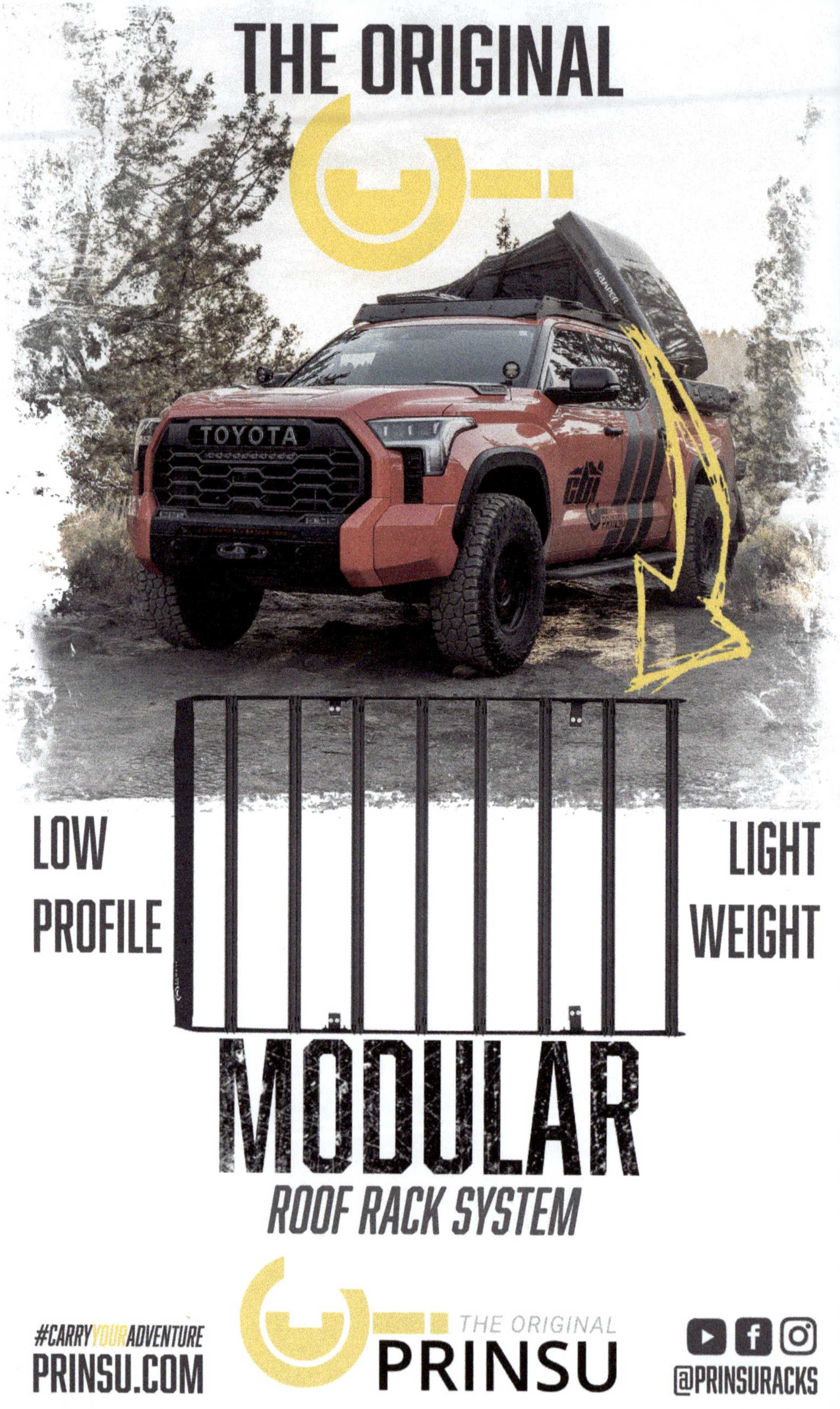

THE ORIGINAL

MODULAR
ROOF RACK SYSTEM

LOW PROFILE

LIGHT WEIGHT

Love These Routes?

Without Your Help,
They Might Survive Only as a Memory

Scan This Code or Visit www.UtahPLA.com/help/ To Help Us Save Them

UPLA

UTAH PUBLIC LANDS
ALLIANCE

Inman Pass
Inkom, ID

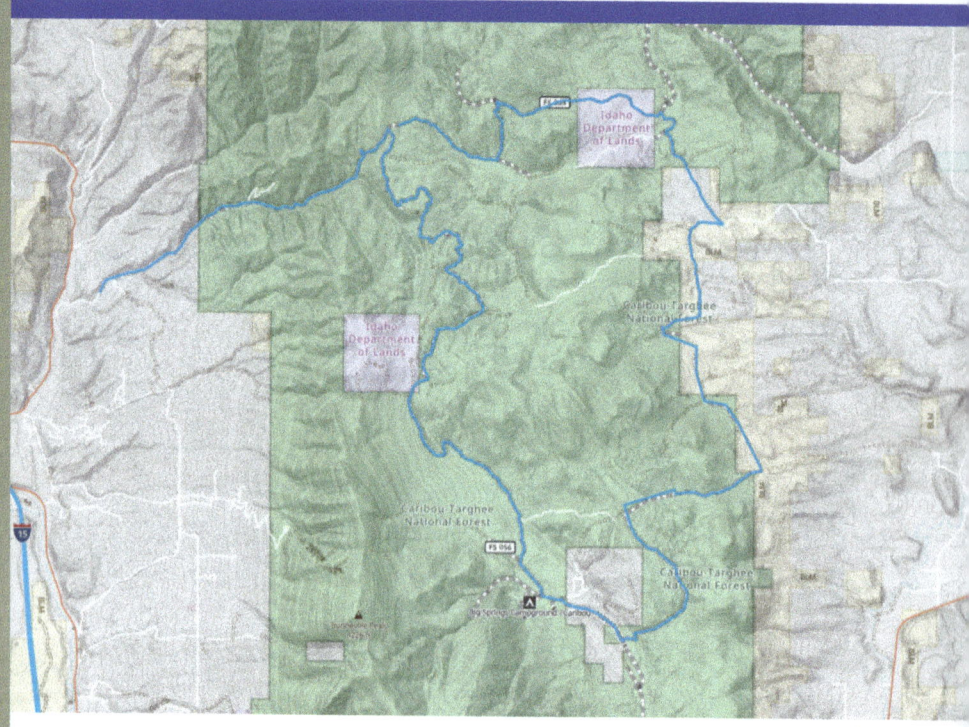

This trail can be accessed from multiple directions, but the preferred offroad route is coming in from the west off East Inman Rd. The access to this collection of trails is a closure hazard. On the east side there are several crossings into BLM land that are used for grazing and fuels collection. This will almost definitely be an issue in the upcoming TMP. It is in no way a secret trail, but rather a home to the locals to exercise their rights to public lands with every modality from hiking to full-size present.

The main road can be run with little frustration, with the exception of route 70208, this little gate keeper can be rough on your rig. While tire size is not important, a set of lockers would improve your chances of completion dramatically. After you make it up the wall and over the hill, it is a very casual ride. Inman Canyon holds every biome, from dusty desert, dense forest, and mountain peaks, leaving you in awe. If you look closely you will find a marsh right next to a tucked away waterfall at the Big Springs Campgrounds.

Big Springs Campground is nestled into Long Gulch accessible from the Pebble Creek rec area if you choose to not take the trails routes. These spots are dry and big enough for a small camper with an extra parking lot for your tow vehicles or extra toys. It even has a well-maintained vault toilet. Per usual,

the concern with this area is a level of too much access. The roads cross state, BLM, private, and even Fish and Game. With so many entities being affected, someone is going to have a complaint.

Getting there: Through the heart of Inkom take North Rapid Cr until you come to East Inman Rd and take a right. Up a few miles East Inman Rd comes to an end at the trail head. The coordinates for the air down spot is 42.83917, -112.17747 this is the preferred air down spot and trailer drop is just before the gate to the right. This is a nice safe location to leave your tow rig and map out your run. It even has a little flowing creek that the dogs and kids love to play in.

Trail Guide: Inman Pass NFS Route 70018

Coordinates: 42.8236, -112.2092

Length: 35 mi

Difficulty: 2

Trail Type: All modalities

Jackpine-Pinochle Loop
Ashton, ID

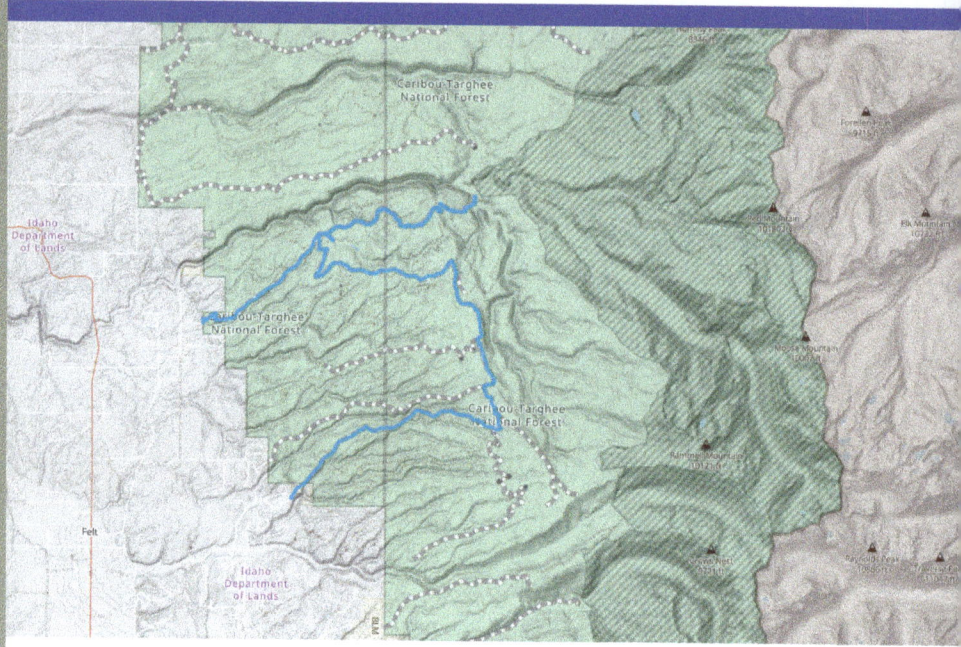

While this is an easy, well-maintained gravel road that any sedan could make it through during the summer, don't be dissuaded. It's a stunning route that heads through the Caribou-Targhee National Forest into Wyoming Teton territory. It follows along the edge of the Jedediah Smith Wilderness with the Grand Tetons as a backdrop. It doesn't get much better for photography than this.

FS 09/Briggs Cabin is a slightly more difficult spur (high-clearance 4x4 recommended) that will take you to an incredible dispersed campsite near Bitch Creek right on the edge of the Wilderness. While not a technical trail, if you're looking for an epic dispersed campsite or picturesque views of the Tetons, bump this to the top of your list.

The trail can be driven in either direction. Starting at the north end and making your way south will present you with a grand unveiling of an incredible vista view of the Teton Range sitting behind the Jedediah Smith Wilderness.

At the trailhead on the north end for Jackpine-Pinochle Loop/FS 266 (43.9399, -111.1299), you'll be welcomed by the Targhee National Forest sign. While we didn't come across any bears, there are plenty of bear signs throughout the Loop— something to keep in mind if you plan on taking your time or camping.

Jackpine-Pinochle Loop is a well-maintained gravel road that cuts beautifully through the Caribou-Targhee National Forest. All throughout the Loop there are plenty of spurs to keep you busy for a couple of days. We explored two of them, one of which leads to an epic campsite on the edge of the wilderness.

FS 658 is a short spur that brings you to a beautiful reservoir being managed for non-motorized use. You will get to a point where vehicles are not allowed (43.9662, -111.0698), but you can enter the area on foot, bike or horse. While we didn't get to hike it, we popped our drone up and can confirm it's a stunning, natural reservoir—worth the adventure if you hike or bike.

Briggs Cabin/FS 09 will lead to an epic campsite alongside Bitch Creek (43.9812, -111.0069) on the border of the Jedediah Smith Wilderness. We highly recommend a high clearance 4x4 for this spur route due to the grade and washouts on the trail. This spur can be deceiving at first. Although not as well maintained as FS 266, 2WD vehicles could make it through most of the route. However, the last quarter mile of the trail gets difficult. While a high clearance 4x4 will have no problem getting down and up, washouts and the grade in the road, which we registered at 18 degrees, would make it very difficult for a 2WD or AWD vehicle with low clearance—especially if wet.

As this spur is less maintained than the main Loop, there are branches and bushes that extend into the trail. Thus, for wider vehicles, expect pinstripes. The trail is also covered in broken trees, thick bark and branches. Some of them could prove problematic for weaker tires if you catch them just right.

If you're not looking to camp, this spur doesn't provide any spectacular views that you'd be missing. However, Bitch Creek is beautiful, and it does get you to the edge of the Wilderness.

If you're looking to camp, this site is spectacular. There is a clearing at the end of the spur right below the trees sitting alongside Bitch Creek that can fit several tents and vehicles. It goes without saying, be sure to respect the laws and regulations of the wilderness designation that sits just beyond the creek.

Back on Jackpine-Pinochle Loop, as you come down the long stretch going south, keep your head up. You'll eventually be presented with a spectacular view of the Teton Range behind Jedediah Smith Wilderness—truly a sight to behold.

Eventually, you'll make it back Tetonia, ID (43.8846, -111.0903). As mentioned, this isn't a technical route. In fact, low-clearance 2WD vehicles could make it through the Loop—but Briggs Cabin would prove difficult. Nonetheless, it's a beautiful and scenic route with some great photo/video opportunities.

Getting There: Start off by making your way through the beautiful farms and ranches of Judkins, ID, just north of Tetonia with the Grand Tetons in the distance. Take ID-32 towards Ashton-Tetonia Trail Idaho State Park. Head east on W 14500N, north on Reece Rd., east on W 14250 N, then north on Wells Ave. which will take you to the start of the Loop.

Trail Guide:Jackpine-Pinochle Loop/FS 266; Briggs Cabin/FS 09

Coordinates: 43.9399, -111.1299

Length: 18+ mi

Difficulty: 1

Trail Type: FS 266 - All Modalities; FS 09 -High Clearance 4x4, Dirt Bike, SxS, ATV, snowmobile

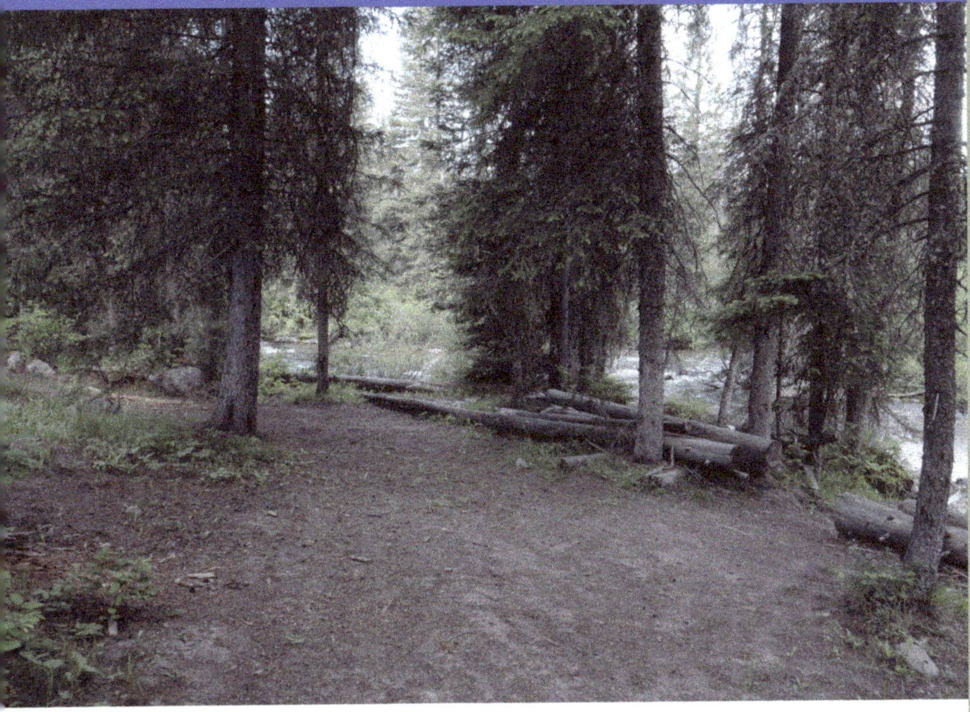

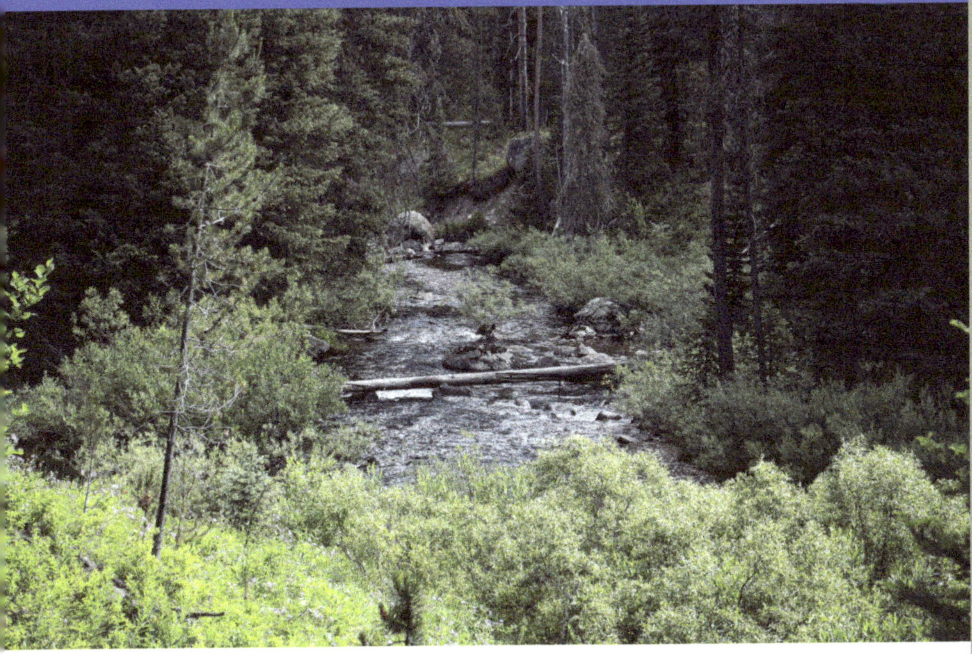

Last Chance Beer Run
Island Park, ID to St. Anthony, ID

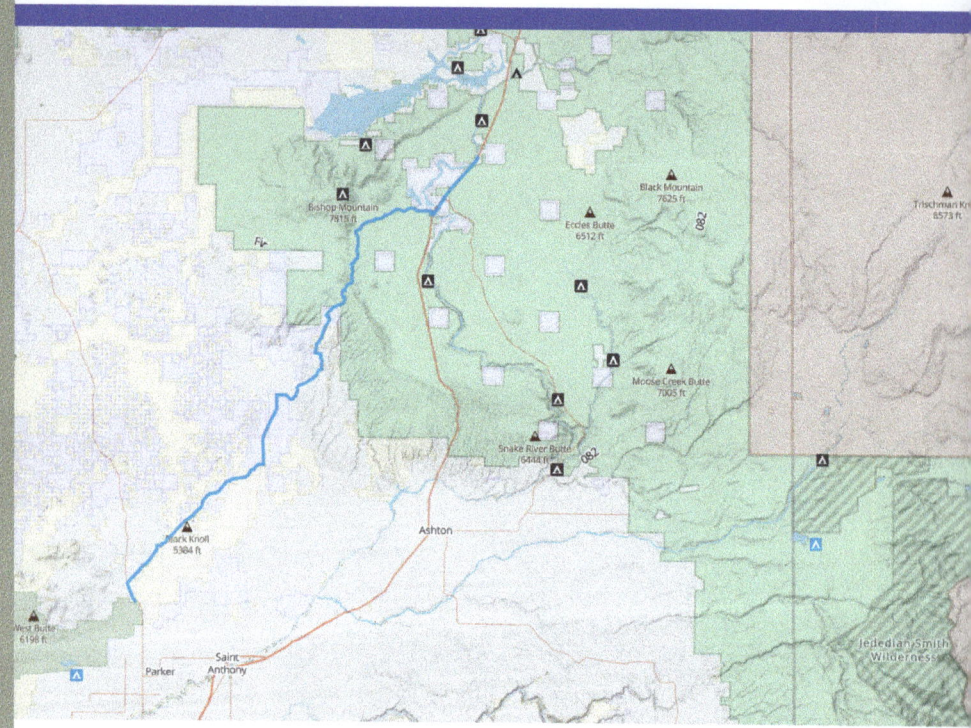

    The Last Chance Trail starts off at the Anglers Inn that sits on the Henry's Fork, just on the outskirts of Island Park. This ride will have a short stint on the highway but soon jumps to the backroads of some of the most amazing roads in Eastern Idaho. You turn off the highway to hit the Beer Run trail and follow that just outside the Herriman State Park, and even go through a small part. If that sounds familiar that is because Herriman and the surrounding area in Island Park, namely the Black Canyon, are being targeted for closures and development pushing recreation of all types out of the canyon year round. This would impact year round recreation for all modalities.

Hang a left on Lyle Spring Stock Driveway 20341 and you will merge with Lyle Springs taking you down through July Creek and some excellent scenic views of the Caribou Targhee outskirts. At different times of years you may see the elk herds running free. In the fall, it is absolutely stunning. Soon thereafter, you will merge back on to the Beer Run trail heading South for another twenty miles ultimately meeting the Red Road. You will drop down ending at the East end of the St Anthony Sand Dunes. This area in the summer is action-packed and usually full of dirt bikes and side by sides.

Different perspectives of the Last Chance Beer Run—snowy and sunny—running from Island Park to St. Anthony, Idaho.

Additionally, this area is also up for the next round of travel management plans. It sits just to the East of the Upper Snake River plan that happened in 2024. Given the sheer amount of trails, counting over a dozen in this section of land, there will surely be an attempt to limit access to numerous trails. So we need everyone to get out on the trail and show their use to their local Clubs and Land Mangers.

Getting there: This run is fairly simple to get to being right off I15 outside of Island Park. There are several parking spots for tow vehicles all around, as well as great accommodations for the out of town crowd.

Trail Guide: Last Chance Trail- NFS, State of Idaho, BLM

Coordinates: 44.363, -111.4028

Length: 41 mi

Difficulty: 2

Trail Type: All modalities

Pausing along the Last Chance trail in southeastern Idaho.

Middle Fork Pass
Lemhi Range, ID

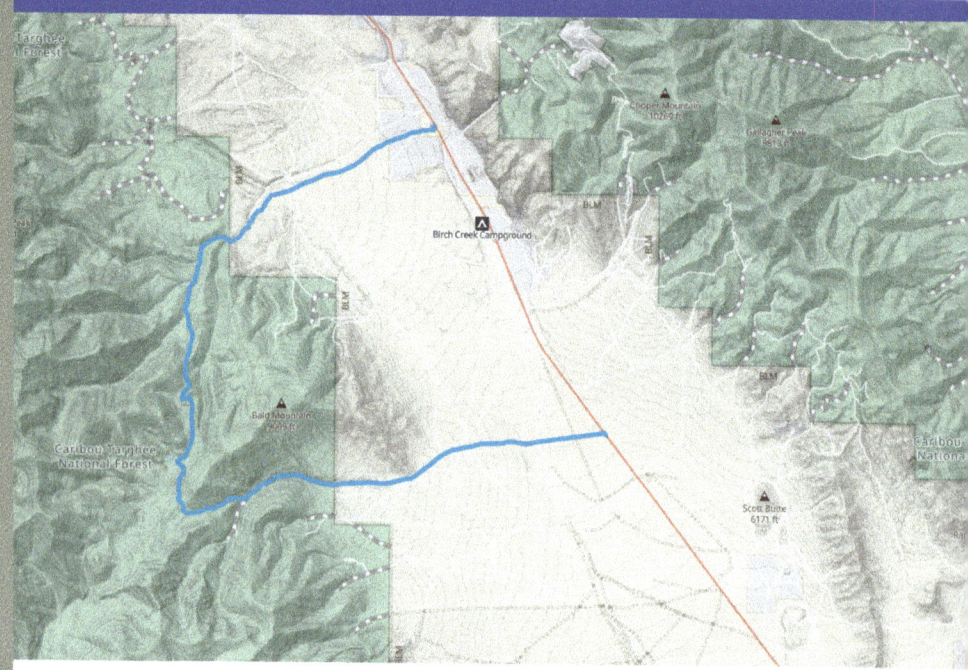

This is a 50" or less only trail. The trail itself is very well defined and is largely non-technical. However, it offers a unique recreation experience in an area where few motorized trails exist that cross the Lemhi Range. With camp sites available at Birch Creek Campground, this area offers a lot to the dirt biker or ATV user looking to spend time in a remote part of Idaho.

The Middle Fork Pass Creek Trail begins at the foothills of the Lemhi Range rising up out of the Birch Creek Valley close to the Birch Creek Campground. At Pass Creek Lake, the trail splits into the Pass Creek Lake Trail and the North Fork Eightmile Trail. If you follow the North Fork Eightmile Trail long enough, you'll find the Uncle Ike Trail. The Uncle Ike Trail will take you across the Lemhi Range to the Pahsimaroi Valley.

Leaving the Birch Creek Campground, there are two options to reach the trail head. You can head north on Hwy 28 before turning west on South Bypass Creek. Follow South Bypass Creek west for about 4.5 miles to find the trail head. The trail head is accessible by full-size vehicles; however, there is a 50" wide gate at the beginning of the trail.

The second option is to cross Birch Creek in the campground and work your way across the Birch Creek Valley towards Bald Mountain Gulch. The water crossing can be difficult to manage depending on the time of year.

The lower section of the trail follows Pass Creek and offers an incredible experience riding through willow trees and massive rock formations. The upper section offers panoramic views of the Lemhi Range and Birch Creek Valley.

Trail Guide: Middle Fork Pass Creek Trail

Coordinates: 44.1616, -112.9208

Length: 5 mi

Difficulty: 4

Trail Type: Dirt Bike, ATV

A rider looking back on the Middle Fork Pass Creek Trail.

Razorback Ridge
Lava Hot Springs, ID

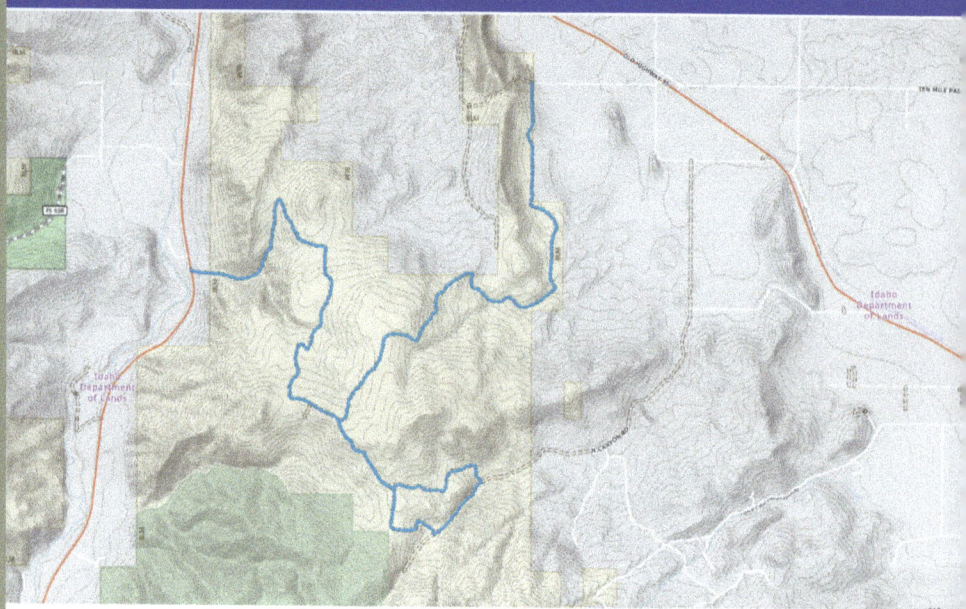

This trail is nestled between multiple mountain ranges on a large swath of BLM land adjacent to the Petticoat Peak Wilderness Study Area. This possesses a particular issue with the expansion of wilderness study areas and closing direct access to trail heads. All four entrances to this trail come from private land and one is already being obstructed by the land owners. Having public land blocked off is becoming more increasingly common. Especially when cattle grazing is prevalent.

While this trail is relatively simple, the views are what you are there for. The ability to look in any direction at every turn, dip, peak, summit, and meadow only to see the next amazing feature the area had to offer. Beginning of the trail off of Old Hwy 3 into N. Canyon is the route we took on this exploration was possibly the most challenging part. We would suggest airing down for comfort, but low gear is hardly needed if at all the entire trip. You will work your way up a canyon with multiple direction changes on a shelf road. Once up top, the trail opens up to those sights that we mentioned. we suggest going back down the canyon to start Razorback Ridge from the bottom. This is where you may have some issues with the trail. The washes are deep and off camber. If it has been raining in the last few days we would avoid this area.

Here you will find a spectacular open area butted up against a massive tree line. Perfect for overland camping or a great picnic. This begins the proper Razorback Ridge, you will climb your way up a steady incline cresting multiple times with several

non designated routes appearing. Please stay on the trail. After the awe settles, you have to work your way off the top of the ridgeline. You get to choose your exit from here, one more scenic and one more rough. Be sure to leave gates as you find them.

Getting there: There is nothing to find on this trail. It is just North East of Lava Hotsprings. If you are passing through on Hwy 30, shortly outside town you will go North on Blasser Rd. If you are looking for a great little camp spot that is not within the bustle of Lava Hotsprings proper right here you will find Portnuff Bend Campground. They even have side by side rentals from Lava Outdoor Fun Rentals if you want to explore the massive side by side trail network in the area. Keep going North about 7 miles to N Canyon, take a right, and make sure you leave the gate like you found it. From there, happy exploring!

The trail on Razorback Ridge near Lava Hot Springs, ID.

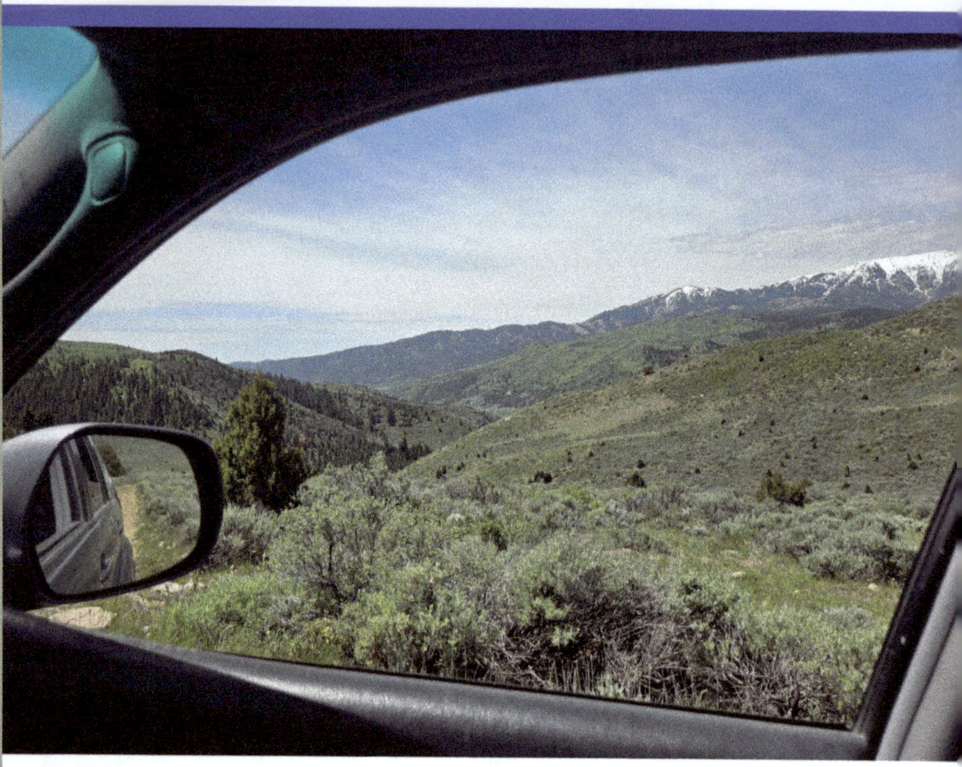

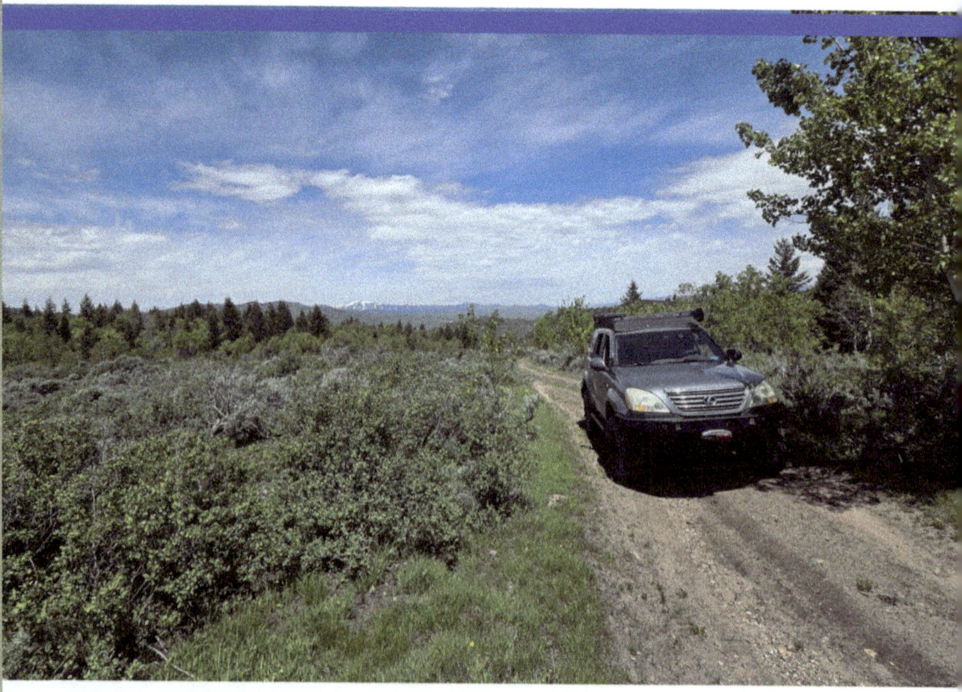

Trail Guide: Razorback Ridge, BLM

Coordinates: 42.73240, -111.99857

Length: 8-11 mi

Difficulty: 2

Trail Type: All modalities

Sedgewick Pass
Downey, ID

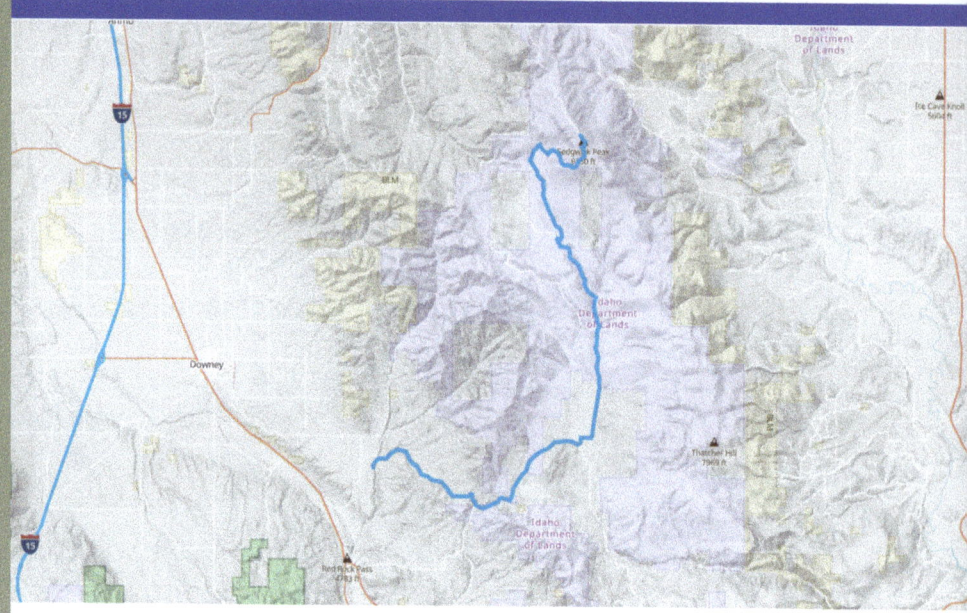

Depending on which way you approach the trail gives you two completely different experiences. As of 2025 there are no designations for the trails leading to Sedgewick Peak so your modality is not limited. But, it should be questioned! While not overly difficult for the majority of the trails, rocky and rutty surfaces make this a thrill ride for your kids or pets. After the casual trail comes some slightly challenging components that test your desire to finish said trail.

Coming in from the South your main thoroughfare is Cottonwood Rd that eventually ends within reach of the trail system. Along your way up Cottonwood, you will have many opportunities for dispursed camping and even large group sized sites for big hunting trips with your buds. If you are an overlander and out for a weekend stroll you may want to stop and camp at this spot (42.37284, -111.98727) this is a super secret spot with views that will shock you. After you make your way up the creek road, that is when the ruckus begins.

The climb up the side of Sedgewick is chock-full of loose basketball sized rocks, fallen trees and limbs, and even banks of snow well into the late spring early summer. The off camber situations while eyeballing that tree you may or may not wind up laying on or puncturing a tire is part of the allure! There will be multiple tight corners that need to be navigated gently with anything over a large side by side with very little room for turning around and no room for oncoming traffic. It is spectacular and pristine, so please do your part to keep it that way!

Getting there: Off of US 91 do yourself a favor and drop down to Swan Lake and check out the cute little mercantile shop at the corner of 91 and Cottonwood Rd. It's your last stop for a restroom and food for a while. From there head East on Cottonwood Rd and take it straight up into the trail system. There is a lot of grazing in the area so be aware of those blind corners.

Trail Guide: Sedgewick Pass, Idaho Department of Lands

Coordinates: 44.16001, -112.91291

Length: 17-20 mi

Difficulty: 2

Trail Type: SXS, Full Size, Motorcycle

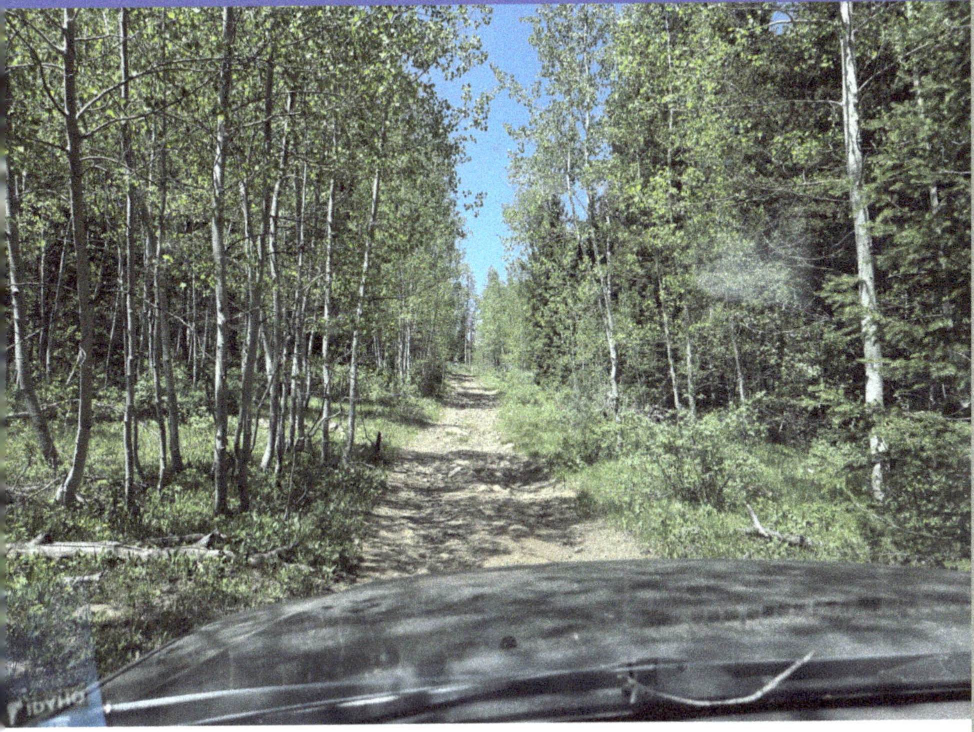

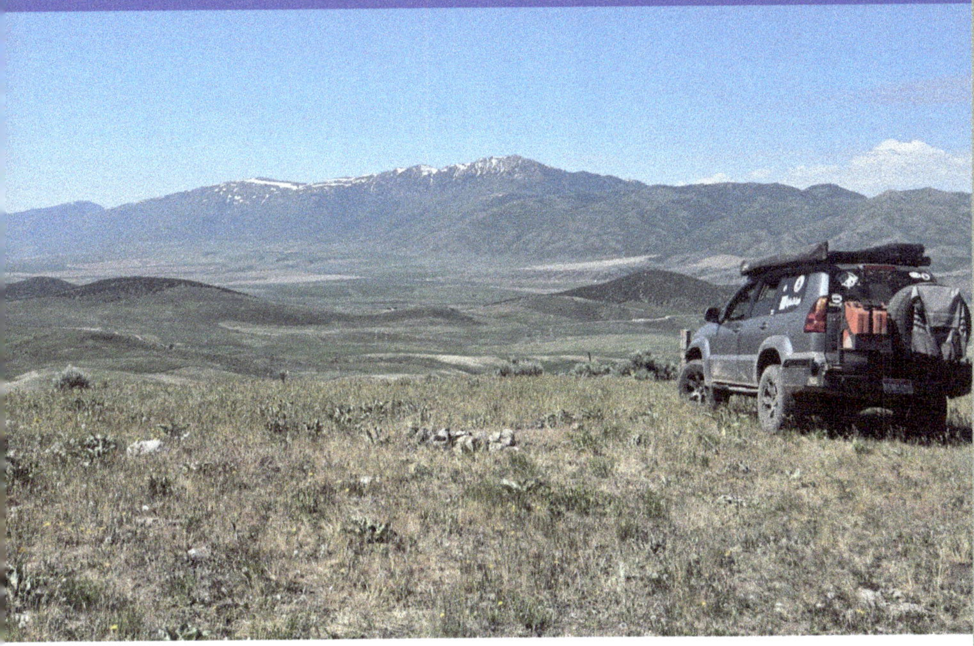

Making the way up the Sedgewick Pass trail.

WINTER 4×4 JAMBOREE

HURRICANE, UTAH

From Mild to Wild Off-Road Trail Runs & Rock Crawling

3RD WEEKEND OF JANUARY

HURRICANE, UTAH

All profits donated to OHV land use and conservation.

For event & registration information visit

www.winter4x4jamboree.com

 RIG SHOW

CATERED DINNER

 HUGE RAFFLE

VENDOR SHOW

Skull Canyon
Lone Pine, ID

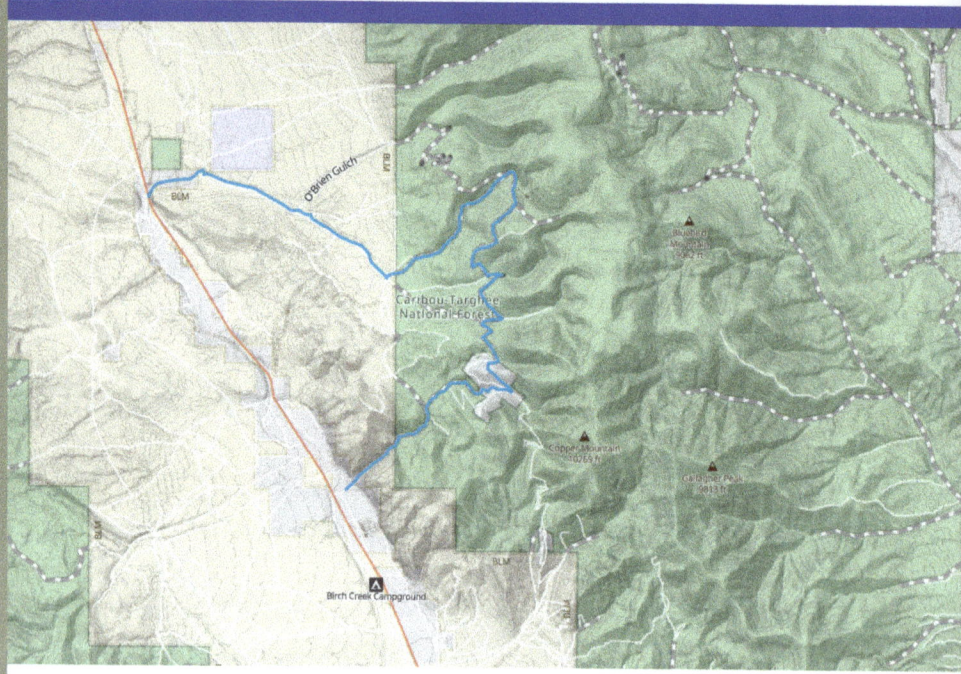

This is a great everyman trail chock-full of history. Shortly after you enter the canyon off the main road, if you look closely up to the left, you will see an ancient system of ladders still hanging on the rock face. Continue winding through the canyon on the right hand side you will find a small cave with a smattering of petroglyphs. Keep to the right you will work your way up a few switch backs that open up to a view between the Lemhi and Beaverhead ranges. The vastness that can be seen is utterly stunning and makes you realize how truly small we are on this planet.

Right around the corner, you hit that moment where you don't know if you will make it out of the trail or not. Use some speed as you turn down the hill and you will be fine. After you catch your breath, you will be heading back down the canyon wall to a special spot for lunch. Here you will find multiple old mining cabins and a mine shaft that you can explore. On the way out you will come across dozens of claims and a few recognizable mines littering the hill sides and old equipment scattered about.

On the way out of the canyon you will happen upon another excellent historical trove of petroglyphs inside a few small cut outs in the hillside. This is a slightly developed area with a small parking area. Atop of the hill across from the cave is an excellent spot for a dispersed campsite. It gives an amazing view of the area and is secluded, though it could be windy. This area is subject to closure in many areas as the trails are all on Forest Service, but the access is on BLM land. Closing down any

multiple access roads would hinder trail rides, mining claims, and indigenous persons from accessing their historical areas.

Getting there: Suitable for all vehicles, there is only one section of the trail that is precarious, and that will come about an hour into the ride. You will head North West towards Leadore on Hwy 28 from Mud Lake, just outside of the expansive dispursed camping area known as Birch Creek. Take a right on Skull Canyon through a little bit of private property, please leave the gate as you found it. This will lead you into a marvelous piece of Idaho history that is only accessed from BLM land, so if closed will never be seen again. Go see it as soon as possible and make some memories!

Trail Guide: Skull Canyon 10298

Coordinates: 44.16001, -112.91291

Length: 17-20 mi

Difficulty: 2

Trail Type: SXS, Full Size, Motorcycle

Stroud Lake
Leadore, ID

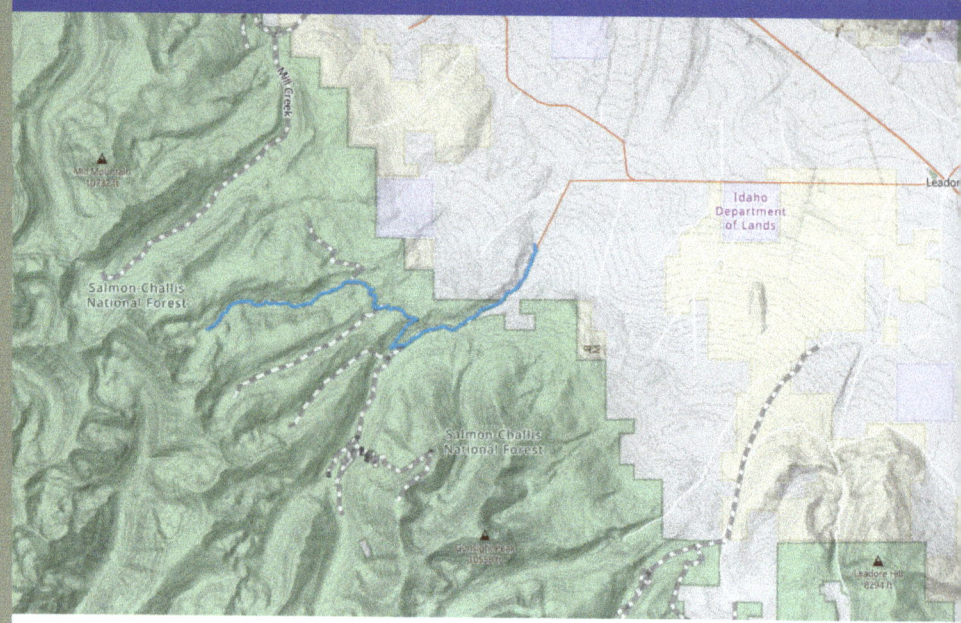

Stroud Lake is the crown jewel of Leadore's three lakes. This will be the challenge of the day, this trail has large rocks in the trail, fallen trees year round, and is very tight. Pinstripes are implied on this trail, for sure. Working your way up the mountain keeps you on edge. Several ledges appear out of nowhere while you are trying not to lose a mirror on the other side of the vehicle.

While a built Jeep is not needed to complete this trail, I would not take a larger overland vehicle for fear of damage—which is a shame because the beach at the lake is an amazing spot to camp! The end of the trail leads out onto the beach which is perfectly flat and not nearly as rocky as the others.

These trails of the Three Lakes need to be protected at all cost. They have already developed the campgrounds at the base of the mountain, if they were to develop these trails for mass use, there would be no character to them.

Closures of this type—of one-way-in trails to bodies of water —have been the target of many closures in recent years because just closing it off to everyone means it will never be harmed. We would much rather work with land managers to keep access open to all on these public lands. What is the point of having this land if no one can see it?

The calm, tranquil waters of Stroud Lake near Leadore, ID.

Getting there: Go West out of Leadore on Lee Cr to Big Eight Mile Rd and turn left. The coordinates for the turn off are 44.63989, -113.55000 to Everson and Stroud Cr the road is marked 64004. Stay on past the Everson trail and you will come upon a left turn off for Stroud 6007.

Trail Guide: FS Route 6007, Stroud Lake

Coordinates: 44.6646, -113.5041

Length: 3 mi

Difficulty: 3

Trail Type: Suitable for all modalities

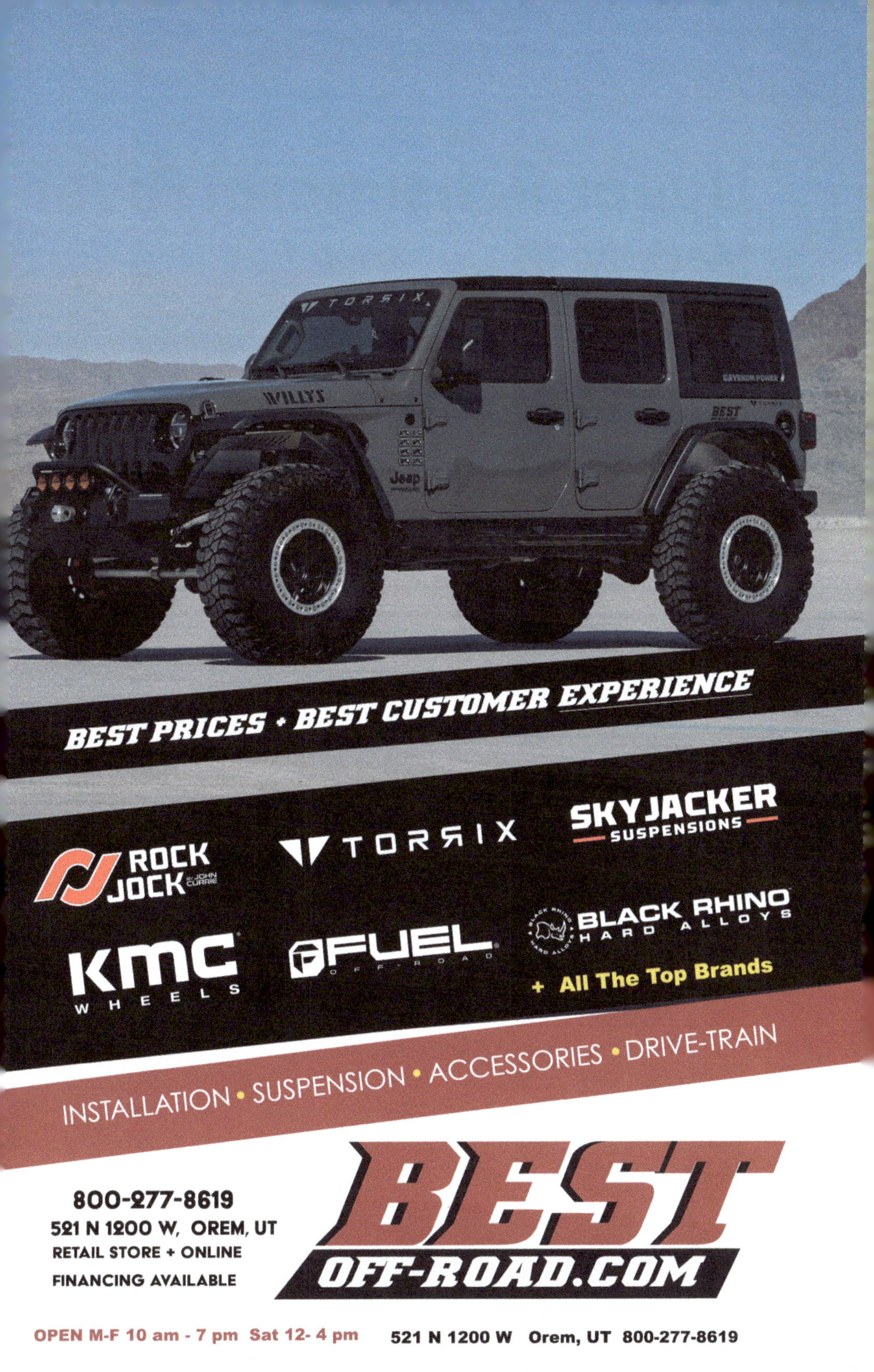
BEST PRICES + BEST CUSTOMER EXPERIENCE
ROCK JOCK BY JOHN CURRIE
TORXIX
SKYJACKER SUSPENSIONS
KMC WHEELS
FUEL OFF-ROAD
BLACK RHINO HARD ALLOYS
+ All The Top Brands
INSTALLATION • SUSPENSION • ACCESSORIES • DRIVE-TRAIN
800-277-8619
521 N 1200 W, OREM, UT
RETAIL STORE + ONLINE
FINANCING AVAILABLE
BEST
OFF-ROAD.COM
OPEN M-F 10 am - 7 pm Sat 12- 4 pm
521 N 1200 W Orem, UT 800-277-8619

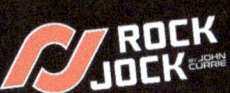

Upper Pahsimeroi River
Mackay, ID

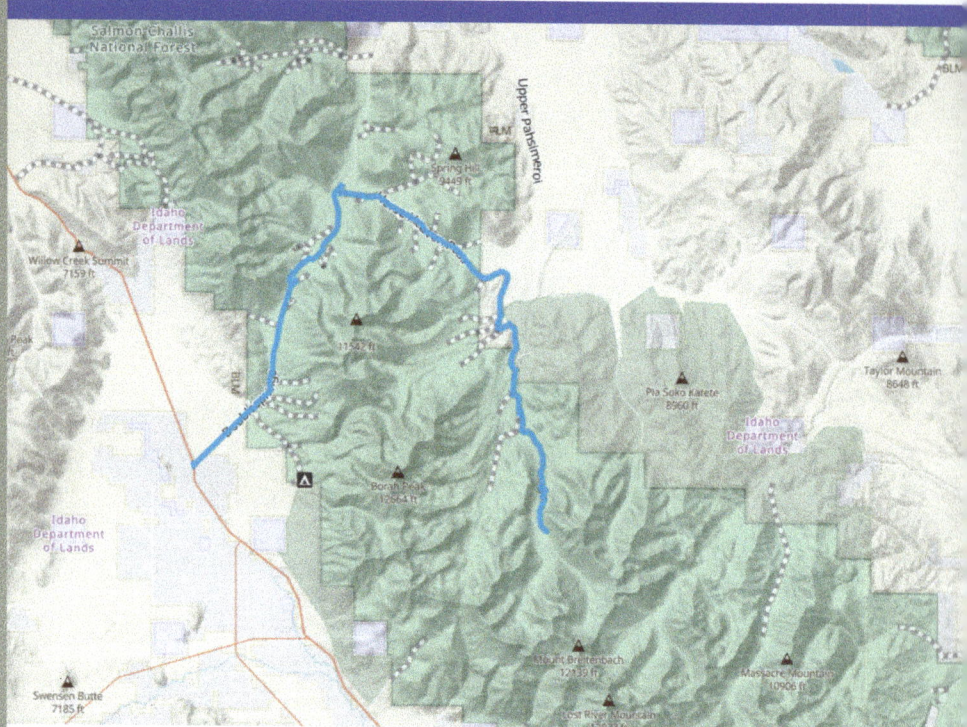

Just past Mackay, Idaho as you drive in the shadow of Mt. Borah—Idaho's tallest mountain—you find the trailhead for Doublespring Pass. This well-maintained dirt road accessible by 2WD vehicles is the gateway into the heart of the Lost River Range. But don't let this well-maintained road fool you. The deeper you get into this range, the more off-road capability you're going to want.

After 10.5 miles on this maintained road, you will find a junction with Horse Heaven Pass. As you veer eastward and deeper into this rugged country, you start to find numerous spur roads that lead to exquisite dispersed campsites and backcountry adventure routes. While it was tempting to explore each and every side road that ventured into the deep woods or straight up mountains, it is worth pressing on to get to the Pahsimeroi River drainage.

The Upper Pahsimeroi River Road connects with Horse Heaven Pass and takes you due south into a river drainage that drains off the north face of Mt. Borah. Along the way we encountered deer, antelope, and even a moose at one of the trail water crossings. This portion of the road became a lot more rugged, but not something a stock 4x4 with good clearance couldn't handle.

Eventually the Upper Pahsimeroi River road forks, and we veered to the East when scouting this trail. This brought us into a valley with 12,000 foot mountains surrounding us on all sides. Even though the day of our excursion into this deep Idaho backcountry was veiled with wildfire smoke from fires hundreds of miles away, the smoke only added to the mystique of these looming mountains. Eventually the road ends and gives access to hiking trailheads for those who want to explore deeper into this country.

While this trail isn't under immediate threat of closure, it is the kind of road that has the potential to be closed through future wilderness designations. It is also the kind of road that shows how important it is to have motorized access into the backcountry to make a range of other activities available.

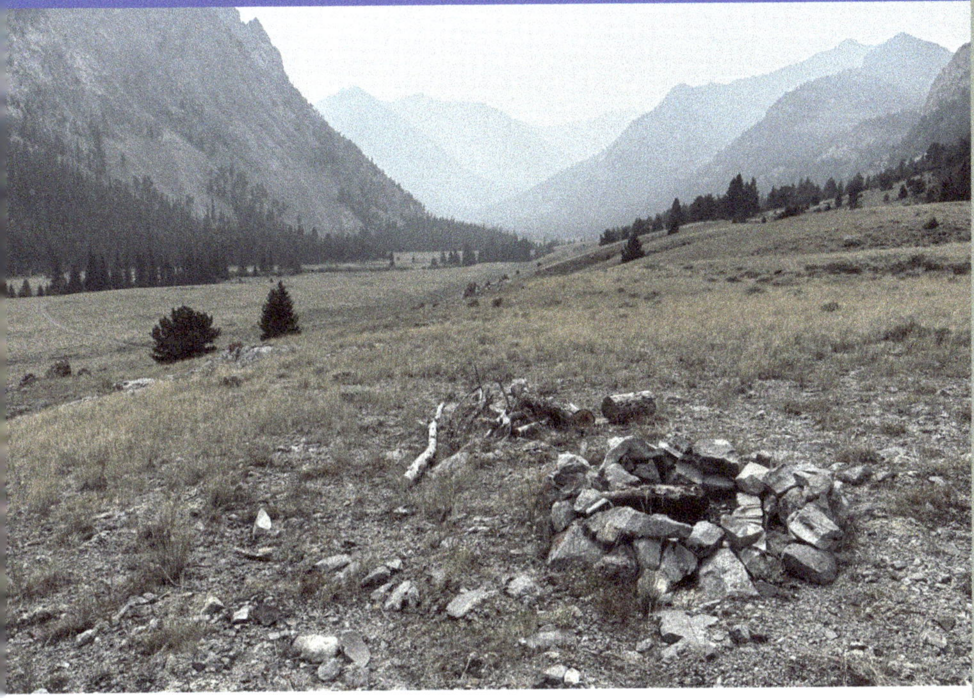

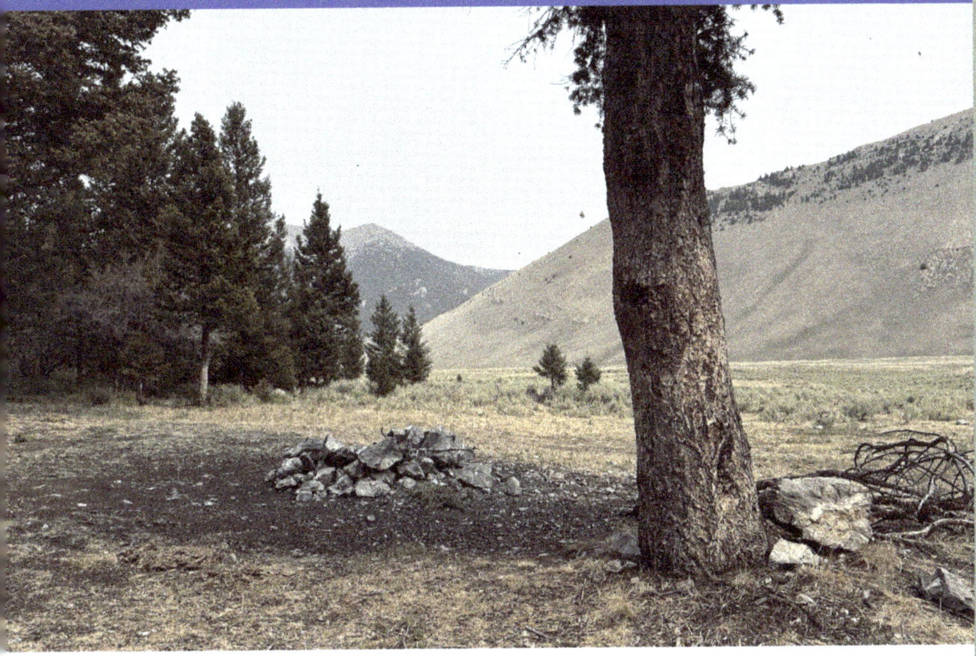

Trail Guide: Double Springs Pass; FS 40118 Upper Pahsimeroi River

Coordinates: 44.1406, -113.9045

Length: 26.5 Mi

Difficulty: 5

Trail Type: Suitable for all modalities (SXS, Full-Sized, etc.)

Whether you're hunting, riding horses, hiking, camping, or just exploring for the day, roads like this embody everything we're fighting for at BRC.

We would like to thank our friends at CBI Off-road for guiding us into this area for a day, so we could strengthen our resolve to fight for Idaho's trails.

The open trail along the Upper Pahsimeroi River route.

Massacre Rocks
Lone Pine, ID

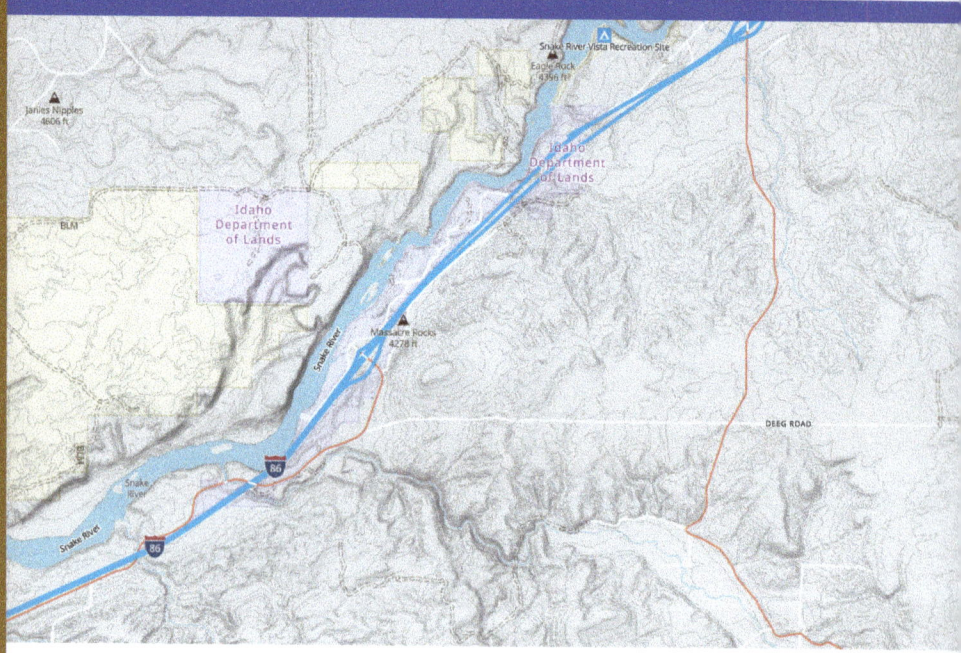

If you've ever driven I-86 in southern Idaho on your way from Pocatello to Boise, you've probably seen the vast lava flows and rugged canyons near Massacre Rocks. The scenic stretch of highway is defined by the Snake River as it winds through a landscape shaped by fire, water, and time. For generations, this area has been a place where people come to climb, ride, camp, and explore.

For years, the BlueRibbon Coalition has stood with the families, climbers, and off-road riders who call this country home. One of our founders rode his dirt bike here on trails that had been here for years. Earlier plans that closed some of these trails prompted Clark Collins to start BlueRibbon Coalition (BRC) to counter the efforts to close off our public lands. These canyons, boulders, and basalt walls are woven into the story of who we are —Idahoans and Americans who believe public lands should be shared and enjoyed responsibly by everyone.

But in recent years, the Bureau of Land Management made a subsequent decision that threatens to erase that legacy. Under the banner of protecting cultural resources in the American Falls Archaeological District, BLM moved to close the Massacre Rocks area to OHV use and rock climbing. The decision came after a planning process that dragged on for more than a decade. This deficient process relied on old public input and ignored key stakeholders like the recreation community.

At first glance, protecting sacred sites and artifacts sounds noble. We agree that these places deserve respect and care. But the way the agency handled this process tells a different story. Instead of bringing all sides together to find balanced solutions, BLM built the plan around a single, narrow vision that shut out anyone who uses a motorized vehicle, climbs a basalt wall, or wants to see multiple-use management of public lands. The National Environmental Policy Act (NEPA) requires federal agencies to evaluate a full range of reasonable alternatives, but here the agency only offered one real choice—the plan to close the area completely. That's not a fair process; it's a foregone conclusion dressed up as public input.

As with many public land closures, this isn't just about trails. It's about ensuring that decisions about our shared lands are made openly, lawfully, and with respect for all the communities that value them. We can protect sacred sites and still allow responsible recreation. We can honor cultural heritage without erasing outdoor traditions that are part of Idaho's story too.

We are including this information about the closure of this iconic area in this guidebook, because we need to create a collective memory of what we've lost. We need to remind ourselves and others, that we belong here, too. We have strong legal standing to challenge this closure, and we are pursuing all legal and political options to get these vital public lands open for all Americans to enjoy.

An example of a climbing route in Massacre Rocks.

Massacre Rocks should be a place where Tribal members, climbers, off-roaders, campers, and families can share the land and its stories. It's time to restore balance, reopen access, and remind the Burearu of Land Management that public lands belong to the public.

If you care about keeping America's open spaces truly open, stand with us. Let's work together to reopen Massacre Rocks.

Tierra Del Sol Four Wheel Drive Club of San Diego (TDS)
Established 1962

When your adventures bring you to San Diego, we invite you to join us on the trail. TDS proudly welcomes guests and encourages anyone with a passion for off-roading to explore membership.
Learn more at tds4x4.com.

For more than six decades, our club has been dedicated to protecting and preserving access to public lands—especially for motorized recreation. We work year-round to keep trails open, support responsible use, and ensure that future generations can enjoy these public lands.

Each March, we host our **Annual TDS Desert Safari**, now celebrating 63 years of off-roading, camaraderie, and family fun. We'd love for you to join us for an unforgettable weekend in the desert.
Event details at tdsdesertsafari.com.

Proceeds from Desert Safari support organizations like the BlueRibbon Coalition and others who advocate for continued access to our public lands.